COME, O HOLY SPIRIT!

by Don Dolindo Ruotolo

Translated by Fr. Peter Damian M. Fehlner, FI

ACADEMY OF THE IMMACULATE

NEW BEDFORD, MA

2007

COME, O HOLY SPIRIT! is a book prepared for publication by the Academy of the Immaculate [academyoftheimmaculate.com], POB 3003, New Bedford, MA, 02741-3003.

FIRST PUBLISHED: Naples, 1949, reprinted 1985.

ENGLISH TRANSLATION: New Bedford, MA, Academy of the Immaculate, 2006

IMPRIMATUR:

Joseph Ma. De Nicola,
Tit. Bishop of Pergamen, Vicar General of Naples
Naples, 21 April, 1949

Cum permissu superiorum

Fr. Stephanus M. Manelli, FI
Minister Generalis
Pentecost, 2007

The permission of the superiors is a declaration of the Roman Catholic Church that a work is free from error in matters of faith and morals, but in no way does it imply that she endorses the contents of the book.

ISBN: 978-1-60114-041-8

Front Cover:

The Holy Spirit depicted as a dove in the stained glass window behind the *Cathedra Petri* in St. Peter's Basilica, Rome.

COME, O HOLY SPIRIT!

by Don Dolindo Ruotolo

Table of Contents

Foreword to the Second Edition

When the first edition of this small, but very popular book, was sold out, demand for it was such as to necessitate a new edition, unchanged except where account has been taken of the revised rite for administration of the Sacrament of Confirmation and current devotional prayers to the Holy Spirit.

Typographically, the lay-out of the new edition sets the various sections of the book and the respective chapters of each section in greater relief. Rather than a second edition, this volume should, strictly speaking, be classed as a reprint, insofar as the text composed by Father Dolindo has remained unaltered.

The author, who has always focused his innumerable writings on the majesty of God, on the Eucharistic and crucified Jesus, and on Our Lady, also finds in the Holy Spirit a key axis for his extraordinarily profound spirituality.

We need only recall his *Veni, Sancte Spiritus*, a work of 348 pages (33 meditations or elevations of the soul of the priest to the Holy Spirit: *elevatio mentis sacerdotalis seu 'sursum cordis' sacerdotis in Deum*),[1] originally part of a book written for priests,[2] substantially dogmatic in content, yet in the delicately balanced style of a lofty, contemplative teaching.

In this work, *Come, O Holy Spirit*, an indisputably orthodox theology is simply and clearly presented, uplifting the soul in authentically ascetical and mystical meditations. It is a work addressed to and particularly useful for those preparing for Confirmation, for catechists, and for all who wish to deepen the vivifying presence of the Holy Spirit in their souls and make him the very light of their existence.

---

1   3rd edition, Naples 1998
2   *Nei raggi della grandezza e della vita Sacerdotale*, Meditations for priests, Naples, 1938, pp. 471–637 (*imprimatur* dated 1938), reprinted 1940, now in its third edition.

When the first edition of this book appeared in 1950, the Rev. Father Philip da Boriello, at the time Provincial of the Capuchins, wrote as follows: "I exhort Fr. Ruotolo to print thirty million copies of this book, *Come, O Holy Spirit,* so that a copy might be given to every Italian: it would mean the Christian renewal of Italy…"

Naples, November 19, 1985

Fifteenth anniversary of the death of Don Dolindo

Translator's Note

Although written nearly sixty years ago, well in advance of Vatican II, this little work of Don Dolindo Ruotolo anticipates the very best, theoretically and practically, in what theologians call a renewed interest and stress on "pneumatology" or the person of the Holy Spirit in the economy of salvation, a presence and operation intimately and uniquely bound up with that of the Immaculate Virgin as Mother of God and Mother of the Church. From a purely practical standpoint, one need only glance at the chapter on the charisms of the Holy Spirit to appreciate the soundness and foresight of the author, whose cause for canonization is being actively promoted by the Archdiocese of Naples and the Franciscans of the Immaculate. Those seeking an authentic participation in the spirituality of Pentecost, of living their anointing by the Spirit of Christ in Baptism/Confirmation, will not be disappointed in this book.

In content and layout, the English translation conforms to the most recent Italian edition. Here and there, brief explanatory footnotes have been added by the translator, indicated by a [Tr. note] at the end of the note. Within the text, scriptural references and/or allusions have been supplied, without comment, where absent in the Italian editions.

Marian Friary, New Bedford, MA, November 21, 2006

A Word of Presentation

Whoever reads the few instructions of the Catechism on Confirmation will immediately grasp that this Sacrament serves to form *perfect Christians and soldiers – knights of Jesus Christ*. But if one observes the mass of Christians today, one must admit that a large number reveal themselves to be anything but perfect Christians and soldiers of Jesus Christ, in spite of having received the Sacrament of Confirmation. Their life is simply pagan, and out of human respect they have abased themselves to the point of fighting among the enemies of God. How did this come about? From abysmal ignorance and from the almost total absence of any preparation for the reception of this Sacrament; and it is necessary to add, *from the lack of any care taken to cultivate and render it fruitful after having received it.*

As a help to eliminating these problems, we offer this small volume, both for preparing souls more efficaciously for Confirmation and even more, we can say, to remind those already confirmed of their obligation to cultivate this Sacrament and restore it to life within themselves, so to bear fruit.

Those who receive Holy Communion feel the duty of making a fitting thanksgiving, and only in so doing do they, in fact, enjoy the fruits of the Eucharist. On the other hand, those who receive the Holy Spirit omit the obligatory thanksgiving more often than not, and immediately proceed to engage in excessive celebration; and thereafter, cease to give Confirmation even a passing thought for the remainder of life. Yet, our entire life ought to be a daily thanks to the Holy Spirit come to dwell in us; and every day, we should cultivate and make fruitful his gifts so as not to render his visit vain in practice.

Hence, we are not offering a theological treatise on the Holy Spirit, although what we say is taken from Sacred Theology.

Rather, in an easy form within the grasp of all, we propose to explain, by analogies and parallels, the teaching of the Church on the action of the Holy Spirit in us, on his gifts and on his fruits. Ours is a wide-ranging instruction on Confirmation, aiming at providing souls with their first notions of the quest for perfection in their lives, and for becoming Christians and soldiers of Jesus Christ in their profession of faith. Ours is a wide-ranging and detailed instruction on the action of the Holy Spirit in us, because correspondence with this action in us is the secret for living in a Christ-like manner as true children of the Church. We implore the One and Triune God, through the intercession of the All Holy Virgin Mary, that these humble pages will penetrate the reader's heart and accomplish a bit of good therein.

Naples, March 25, 1949, Solemnity of the Annunciation

Don Dolindo Ruotolo

Introduction

✑

I. A Common Complaint

Any right-living soul, that is, one living to glorify God and to do good, will notice the decline of Christian life and strongly feel its effects. Today, Christians are, indeed, an absolute majority in Italy and many take pride in this. It is, however, an undeniable fact that some are perverse, and as such, are actively aggressive within the Church, and in consequence, very dangerous to the Faith. The Christian majority does not succeed in overcoming or eliminating this hostility, despite the fact that a considerable number work zealously to accomplish that very goal. Why is this so? When an organism does not succeed in rejecting a sickness or infection that might afflict it, it is considered to be a weak and torpid organism. Antibiotics are vigorously administered and all forms of advanced medical technology are employed to overcome the infection, yet in spite of this, well-being is not restored because the organism is in such an advanced, weakened condition, life itself is wanting. As a result, the illness is virulent, invasive, and life-threatening.

This describes exactly what is happening to the modern world: life-threatening infections spread rapidly, but the healthy part which should react, either does not, or reacts insufficiently. The evil spreads; the people are corrupted; patterns of living decay and turn barbaric; immorality, impurity, anger, thievery, oppression, and murder team violently, like malignant tumors. All this virulence ends either in social upheaval or wars.

WHEN PHYSICIANS BECOME aware of a progressive malignancy, they seek out the cause in order to overcome or eliminate it altogether, using every modern method of diagnoses available, no matter the cost: analyses, chemical tests, cat-scans, x-rays, lumbar punctures, surgeries, etc. What is the cause of Christian decay and of its virulence? It is the lack of Christian spirit, and consequently, of Christian life. From where does this originate? A sickness is always the result of a malfunctioning, perhaps of the liver, of the heart, of the lungs, of the circulation, or of the brain. If this disorder is not remedied, the illness will advance. In Christian life, there exists a grievous malfunction which brings about this decay and which, seemingly, no one notices: *the supernatural life of Christians is impoverished, and absolutely wanting of the Holy Spirit.* Christians don't have a clue as to what Christian life is about, and are neither animated by grace nor by the gifts of the Holy Spirit. This is an undeniable fact, perfectly evident from the manner in which the majority receives the Sacrament of Confirmation. This vivifying Sacrament is approached in the greatest ignorance, and a clear symptom of this ignorance is the absence in bookstores of even a small work shedding full light on this Sacrament.[3]

Confirmation is received in haste without proper dispositions of any kind, merely to obtain the required certificate for the marriage contract in the future. Prospective recipients distractedly approach this Sacrament in a state of dissipation, chatting and laughing, with more concern for the

---

3 The comment of Don Dolindo is in reference to the situation in Italy in the late 40's of the last century, in reference to solid and practical Catholic commentary on the gifts of the Holy Spirit and Christian life in the Spirit as fruit of the Sacrament of Confirmation. Curiously, the situation is not much different today as regards practical manuals on Confirmation as a basis for the cultivation of the interior life of the Christian, despite the increased number of works on the Holy Spirit in general and his charisms in particular. On the broader subject of the Holy Spirit and the cultivation of the interior life, there are a number of classic works available in English: the two volumes of Cardinal Manning on the interior and exterior mission of the Holy Spirit (19th century works) and the 20th century works: *The Spirit and the Bride* by Abbot Vonier (London 1937) and *The Holy Ghost* by E. Leen (New York 1939). [Tr. note.]

celebration to follow and the gift from their sponsor, than for the ineffable life conferred by the Holy Spirit, with his gifts and fruits, to activate and perfect that Christian life.

II. Key Concepts

It is not possible to form a clear idea of the action of the Holy Spirit in us without certain basic concepts which make it easy to understand this action. Anyone, for example, who seeks to activate a machine, must have some grasp of its component parts, their movements and the way to make them function. Now if this is necessary for work involving machines, it is even more so for the work of grace in us that we know the remote and proximate principles governing the action of God in the soul, and the nature of Christian life which is the objective for the sake of which the Holy Spirit comes into us and vivifies us with his grace and with his gifts. Let us begin with a glance at ourselves who are the subjects in whom the Holy Spirit works.

We are formed of soul and body. The body lives via its natural development and the activity of its organs. The soul has a *natural* life in the activity of all its faculties, and also enjoys a *supernatural life* communicated to it by the goodness of God: the *life of grace*, or a sharing in the very life of God. This life does not deprive us of our free will. On earth, this life can grow in us and be perfected, just as in a field plants and trees grow from living shoots and bear fruit. Hence, we must *perfect ourselves* throughout the course of our mortal life, according to the state in which God has placed us and the mission we are to fulfill on earth, so as to enrich ourselves with merit and gain eternal life.

The process of becoming perfect entails an inner struggle because, composed of body and soul, united so as to form a single nature and person, our lower powers ardently tend to pleasure, whereas the higher to the good; and so, these powers often find themselves in conflict: flesh against spirit and spirit against flesh; will against passion and passion against will. For this reason, the Holy Spirit calls this life a *warfare.*

The drives of the flesh and of the passions toward sensible pleasures, however, are not irresistible. The will, supported by the intellect, possesses a fourfold power of control over such passionate drives. First – the power of *foresight,* in anticipating dangerous emotions with prudent watchfulness; second – the powers of *inhibition* and of *moderation,* whereby one may forbid the eyes, for example, to look at dangerous images, and may control violent emotion suddenly aroused in the soul, for example, violent rage; third – the power of *stimulus,* to spur on resistance to evil; fourth – the power of *direction,* to guide the activity and drive of the passions toward good.

But a man does not fight this battle with these powers alone. By the goodness of God, he has been raised to a higher state and endowed with preternatural and supernatural gifts which facilitate victorious combat. These gifts come to us from the Holy Spirit through the Redemption and merits of Jesus Christ, unite us with God, enable us to share his divine life, and make us capable of resisting evil and doing good.

An airplane is naturally heavy, indeed very heavy. Its weight forces it violently to the ground. But its wings and motor, with rudder, propellers, and flight instruments enable it to take off, overcoming gravity and launching it into the wide, blue heavens. Something similar happens in us: the flesh weighs us down; the spirit is poised to soar on high, like the extended wings of the airplane. Without the motor, however, the airplane does not move; and without grace our soul does not ascend on high nor does it overcome the weight of matter and of the flesh. Grace is bestowed on us with the sacraments, and so it is necessary to have some notion of these great treasures, given to us by Jesus Christ our Redeemer.

III. General Notions of the Sacraments

The Lord, then, in his great mercy confers on us and increases grace in us by means of the sacraments. A sacrament is *a sensible sign, definitively instituted by Jesus Christ to signify and confer sanctifying grace*. The sacraments are seven: Baptism, Confirmation, the Eucharist, Penance (Reconciliation), Anointing of the Sick (Extreme Unction), Holy Orders, and Matrimony.

Constitutive elements of the sacraments are *the matter and form*. The matter is the element or sacramental sign. The form, or words, pronounced by the minister of the sacrament in applying the matter, determines the meaning of the sign precisely as sacrament, and confers on it the power to sanctify. For example, in Baptism the matter is water, and the form are the words: *I baptize you in the name of the Father and of the Son and of the Holy Spirit*. These words realize the sacrament here and now, and constituted as such, bestow the grace of rebirth and other graces annexed to this.

The sacraments are an immense gift from God because, from birth to death, they sanctify the entire course of life in its every aspect and provide us with the possibility of gaining eternal glory. All of them confer sanctifying or *common* grace, and *sacramental grace*, the grace distinctive of each sacrament. They can confer the first grace when the soul lacks this, as in the case of Baptism, or when the soul has lost grace, as is the case with Penance. They confer an increase of grace when the soul already possesses it, as in the case of the other five sacraments, or in the sacrament of Penance, when the person receiving it is already in the state of grace, because he does not have mortal sins on his soul. If a person in good faith believes he is in the state of grace while approaching the sacraments which require such a state as prerequisite, these sacraments would confer on such a person the first grace, provided the person has in his soul at least attrition for his sins.[4] Anointing of the Sick also confers the remission of mortal sins, when the person receiving this Sacrament is unable to confess his sins.

The sacramental grace proper to each sacrament, over and above sanctifying grace and the increase of sanctifying grace, is that grace corresponding to the special significance of each sacrament, insofar as it has been instituted for a specific purpose. Thus, we are reborn by means of Baptism; by means of Confirmation grace is increased in us and we are strengthened in the faith; through the Eucharist we are nourished supernaturally with the divine food of the Body and Blood of Jesus Christ; with Penance we are reborn to a lost grace; through Anointing of the Sick we are purified and strengthened in the face of death, and also supported in the trials consequent on misfortune and in bodily health, if such should be God's pleasure. Five sacraments are directed toward the spiritual perfection of the soul, while the other two, *Holy Orders* and *Matrimony*, are directed toward government and multiplication of the Church. The nature, then, of sacramental grace *is identical with habitual grace, with the right to special, actual graces corresponding to the distinctive goal of each sacrament.*

Three sacraments imprint a character and cannot be repeated: Baptism, Confirmation, and Sacred Orders. Character *is a spiritual sign and indelible mark on the soul, by which men are oriented toward the things of God and are differentiated among themselves.*

In order to be administered, every sacrament needs a minister, or someone who has the power and authority to administer it. The principal minister is always Jesus Christ who instituted the sacraments, and in whose name and authority

---

4   Attrition is sorrow for one's own sins, motivated supernaturally, for example, by the ugliness of sin or fear of hell, etc., but not directly by the sorrow for having offended God. It is a sorrow less noble and less perfect, because not motivated by the love of benevolence and friendship for God, but by fear; but united with the Sacrament it is sufficient for remitting the sins of the soul.

they are conferred by secondary ministers. The minister may be *ordinary*, when consecrated or deputized by virtue of his office to confer a sacrament; *extraordinary*, when he may confer it only in cases of necessity or by special privilege. Thus, in case of necessity, any man or woman, in possession of their senses, may legitimately, but not solemnly, baptize. In case of necessity also, and under special conditions, a pastor may confirm in virtue of a privilege granted by the Holy See.

IT IS NECESSARY to consider and deepen, by way of example and analogy, one's understanding of the nature and greatness of the sacraments, ineffable gifts of the Redemption, and sure means for harvesting its fruits. Jesus Christ, in fact, has not simply redeemed us, paying by His passion, the debt incurred by our sins, but has enriched us with extraordinary graces to support and to elevate our life throughout its entire course, from birth to death, as already mentioned. He is the Head and we are the members of the Church, His Mystical Body. By means of the sacraments, we directly participate in His life via seven distinct channels irrigating our souls, His mystical field, and rendering them lovely and fruitful in their every power and activity. The graces which He has given us in the sacraments are not a momentary, but a permanent benefaction.

A generous benefactor, desirous of assisting a poor person in such wise as to guarantee him a secure living, takes a sheet of paper from the house of the poor man, addresses it to the bank where he deposits his own wealth, affixes his seal and signature, and offers it to the poor man, so that he himself might visit the bank and request a sum of money. The poor person need do no more than present the note to the banker, countersign the note and receive what he needs. When all has been done in accord with the law, even by the poor man, the withdrawal is no longer an alms, but a right, based on the wealth, which from his labor and sacrifice, the generous benefactor had deposited in the bank.

If I wish to light a candle, I must touch the flame to the wick; if there is no obstacle, e.g., if the wick is not damp and the flame is near enough, surely the intended result will occur and the candle will be lit. Jesus Christ bestows on us the graces necessary for life and for the salvation of the soul with a gift that cannot fail: it is enough to supply the elements ordained by Him to participate in these gifts, and enough not to place any obstacle in order to receive them infallibly.

What is the paper money of a state or an annuity? It is a sensible sign, instituted by the state to indicate its wealth and to make it circulate in relation to the securities held in its vault. Whoever possesses such paper may not disdain it or tear it simply because it is paper, but must carefully guard it, because it is valuable. Anyone who would presume to print paper money on his own authority is a counterfeiter, and his paper money is rendered worthless, because it has no relevance to any securities of the state. If genuine paper money is hidden in a strong-box, for all practical purposes, it loses its value in not circulating. It is not gold; it is not a gem; it is a piece of paper. But if it is put into circulation, its value is restored, and the paper causes the wealth it represents to circulate, otherwise remaining defunct for lack of circulation.

If the paper is torn so as to no longer be recognizable, or if in its printing the ink gave out, or if it was not properly printed, even though printed in view of possessing a certain value, in reality, it is worthless. The wealth exists in the vaults of the state, but the title, *for want of form*, is worthless and incapable of circulation. Something similar happens in the case of the sacraments, sensible signs of that immense wealth, or a title to an annuity to be cashed when one has encountered or endured some misfortune.

To enjoy such an annuity, a deposit of funds must have taken place, the paper being but a sensible sign of this; the words printed on the paper a statement of its value; and last of all, the signature and seal of the representative of the state who is, as it were, the minister of that title. To have a sacrament, the prerequisites are the rich merits of Jesus, and hence, its divine institution: the sensible sign which expresses the communication of His wealth; the formulary which determines its value; and the minister who acts in the place of Jesus Christ and in His name, distributes the riches of His merits. An alteration or absence of one of these constitutive elements nullifies the sacrament, just as no current is produced in charging an electric battery if water is substituted for acid.

From these elementary and facile examples, the soul can, in some way, grasp the real grandeur and riches of the sacraments. Contemplating means of grace so great, expressed with such simple, sensible signs and with words still more simple, the soul can shake from itself that apathy and indifference which so often might smother it. On throwing a switch, or at the touch of a button, one can light thousands of lamps at a great distance and release formidable power. The touch is an act which, of itself, does not reveal such power; it is first necessary to believe this to assess its value. In such wise, he who receives a sacrament does not grasp what light is enkindled in the soul and what power of grace moves it, if he does not believe in the wonderful efficacy of the gift of God.

Among the sacraments, we shall specifically focus our attention here on Confirmation and, above all, on its wonderful effects.

IV. General Notions on Confirmation

Confirmation is a sacrament of the New Law whereby, through the anointing with oil and the imposition of hands by the bishop, the baptized is strengthened in grace and signed as a soldier of Jesus Christ. It is known as Chrism from the matter used in its conferral, or *Sacred Chrism* – a mixture of oil and balsam, especially blessed by the Bishop on Holy Thursday – and is called *Confirmation* because of the effects it produces in one who receives it in being confirmed and strengthened in the Faith by a particular grace of the Holy Spirit.

The matter of this Sacrament is the Sacred Chrism, the imposition of the hands of the bishop on those to be anointed and the actual anointing which he makes on their foreheads. The Sacred Chrism, before the actual anointing of the confirmands, is called *remote matter*, namely still at a distance and not yet applied. In this matter, the oil denotes the grace which is poured into the Christian to confirm him in the Faith; the balsam mixed with it is sweet-smelling and preserves from corruption, and so signifies that the life of a Christian must give off the pleasing scent of virtue and be preserved from the corruption of vice.

The imposition of the hands and the anointing are *the proximate matter*, or sensible sign of the Sacrament. With the action whereby the soul is anointed, it receives the Holy Spirit with his seven gifts, of which we shall speak at great length. The soul, as it were, is enlisted in the army of Jesus Christ, and precisely when its life develops and meets with the perils of temptation, the soul is strengthened and receives the grace to combat these perils and remain faithful in the state and mission to which God has called it. Even babies in danger of death, who receive this sacrament before attaining the use of reason, obtain the grace of the Holy Spirit, so that, at least with the suffering they endure in dying, they might be active for the glory of God and adorn themselves with a greater claim on glory.

Confirmation must be received by every Christian on reaching the age of reason. It is not a sacrament absolutely necessary for salvation, or as the theologians say, it is not necessary by a *necessity of means* for salvation. But it is necessary by a *necessity of precept*, because this is required by the laws of the Church. For the rest, it is in the best interest of the soul to receive this Sacrament, because without it, the Christian resembles an unarmed soldier lacking any kind of support, exactly when life is at its most perilous. If Jesus Christ has given us this treasury of grace to sanctify and save us, who can overlook or minimize its importance without being guilty of sin?

To receive the sacrament of Confirmation, it is necessary to be baptized and to be instructed in the principal truths of the Catholic Faith, because one cannot defend a faith of which one is ignorant. It is also necessary to know, by heart, all the principal prayers: *Our Father, Hail Mary, Creed, Acts of Faith, Hope, Charity,* and *Contrition,* etc., because a Christian, fighting for Jesus Christ and for the Faith, without the weapons of combat, which are prayers, is inconceivable! Whoever is confirmed, must be in the state of grace, and so must confess and receive Communion. He must also have the intention, at least implicit, of receiving the Sacrament. If he receives Confirmation in the state of sin, he is validly confirmed, but commits a sacrilege, and is deprived of the graces and gifts of the Holy Spirit. These effects of sanctification remain suspended in him so long as he does not confess his sacrilegious act, and thus, make reparation for having committed that sin.

V. Nature of Christian Life

By receiving the sacrament of Confirmation, one becomes fully Christian and a soldier of Jesus Christ, not in act however, because Christian perfection is acquired little by little with the exercise of virtue, and one is a soldier of Christ when, in fact, one joins the combat in defense of the Faith.

In all truth, one should never believe that Christian life consists in having some sacred image in one's home or wallet; or in reciting some prayer more or less distractedly; or perhaps in attending the Holy Sacrifice negligently, engaging in curious and flighty chatter to compensate for having to be present; or at other times, receiving Communion reluctantly. These things are superficial acts and manifestations of Christian life, minimal at best, but are not the life itself.

Christian life is thus defined by theologians, the teachers of supernatural truth: *a participation in divine life, conferred by the Holy Spirit who dwells in us in virtue of the merits of Jesus Christ, and which we must cultivate in the face of tendencies opposing it.* Being a *participant in divine life,* is supernatural life; and, therefore, is a life in which it is necessary to utilize *the gifts of God* to live in God and for God, to live in intimate union with Jesus Christ, and to imitate Him.

Because we do not immediately cease to be miserable and feel inclined toward evil due to a triple concupiscence in us, we cannot participate in divine life without combating this evil within ourselves and overcoming it. This combat is the exercise of virtue. It makes us grow in God through meritorious acts, and makes us feel the need of prayer and of the sacraments, which unite us to God and prepare us for the attainment of eternal life. Summarizing Christian life as follows, we will have a clearer concept of it: *God works in us* by dwelling in us, himself, through the Word Incarnate, through Mary Most Holy who is our Mother, and through the Angels and Saints who are our advocates. *We live and work through God* – fighting against concupiscence, the world, and the devil – sanctifying our actions, praying, and worthily receiving the Holy Sacraments.

God, as St. Thomas says [*Summa,* I, q. 8, a. 3], dwells naturally in his creatures: *by his power,* because all are subject to him; *by his presence,* because he sees all; *by his essence,* because he works everywhere, and because he is the fullness of being and the first cause of all that is real in creatures, continually communicating to them their being, life, and movement.[5] In us Christians, God dwells more particularly by means of *grace,* which is a presence of a much higher and more intimate order. He is not only *in us,* but *he gives himself to us* so that we can enjoy him; he gives himself to us as *Father,* as *friend,* as *collaborator* and as *sanctifier.* He gives himself to us as *Father,*

---

5   The allusion is to a line from the discourse of St. Paul, recorded in Acts 17: 28. [Tr. note]

and we are *his adopted children*, the wonderful privilege that is the basis of our supernatural life. He gives himself to us as *friend*, speaking to us through the Church, and from within, through the Holy Spirit. He gives himself to us as *collaborator*, supplying for our impotence in the supernatural life, with his actual grace, enlightening us, strengthening us, and supporting us. Finally, he gives himself to us as *sanctifier*, bestowing upon us the Holy Spirit with his gifts.[6]

The Christian, then, who remains in the grace of God, and who, by corresponding with that grace, makes the gifts he has received bear fruit, is the temple of the One and Triune God; he is a kind of sacred enclosure reserved to God,[7] a throne of mercy adorned by God with all the virtues. From this throne God is pleased to distribute all his heavenly favors.

VI. Christian Life: Its Organism and General Concept of Gifts of the Holy Spirit

In every life, a threefold element is found: a *vital principle* which is the source of life; *faculties* or powers which stimulate vital activities, and finally *actions* which are its extension and which contribute to its growth. In the supernatural order, God, who lives in us, produces these three elements in our souls: *1)* he communicates to us *habitual grace* which serves in us as *vital supernatural principle* and which divinizes, as it were, the very substance of our soul, making it fit, even if only remotely, for the beatific vision and for those acts which prepare for this vision. *2)* From this grace flow the *infused virtues* and *gifts of the Holy Spirit* which perfect our faculties and which give us the power to perform actions godlike, supernatural, and meritorious. *3)* To set these actions in motion God bestows on

---

6 The summary reflects the synthesis of St. Paul, Gal 4: 4–7, where the entire order of grace is brought into being through the maternal mediation of the "Woman," viz., Mary Immaculate. [Tr. note]

7 The allusion is to the bride of the Canticle of Canticles, 4:12, 5:1, as an enclosed garden reserved to the bridegroom, a figure used to explain the relation of Mary Immaculate, the Church and every holy soul to Christ. [Tr. note]

us *actual graces* which enlighten our intelligence, strengthen our will, help us to work supernaturally, and thus increase the capital share of habitual grace imparted to us by God.

This is the *life of grace* which the Three Divine Persons, dwelling in us, are pleased to communicate to us, enriching us with supernatural gifts. This life, although distinct from natural life, *penetrates the soul in its entirety*, transforming and divinizing it, alikening itself to all that is good in nature, in education, and in habits acquired by the soul. The life of grace perfects and so makes all these elements supernatural, orientating them toward their final end which is the possession of God, by means of the beatific vision and of the love which accompanies it. This is how supernatural life must guide natural life, for the same reason that less perfect beings are subordinated to those who are superior. Supernatural life can neither endure nor unfold, unless it can, in fact, *dominate* and retain under its *influence*, the activity of the intellect, of the will, and of the other faculties. For all this, nature is neither destroyed nor minimized, but exalted and perfected.

It is not possible to live in a Christian way and grow in perfection, without understanding well this organism of the supernatural life, just as it is not possible to start motors or initiate the takeoff of an airplane, lifting it above the earth and releasing it for flight, without knowing well how these machines function. In so many Christians, including souls consecrated to perfection, ignorance of supernatural life is the true cause of that naturalism and of that selfish and materialistic concept of life, which keeps us far from Christian life and perfection, and which accounts for that meager correspondence with the work of the Eternal Love of God in us. The saints are precisely those who have corresponded with grace; have been transformed by grace into new creatures; have been enriched by the generosity and mercy of God; and have been stimulated by his charity to act through a series of uninterrupted, actual graces.

Supernatural life, inserted into our soul by means of habitual grace, requires for its operation and development, powers of a supernatural kind which divine goodness grants us under the names of *infused virtues* and *gifts of the Holy Spirit*. Our natural powers which, of themselves, can produce only natural acts, must be perfected and divinized by infused habits, elevating and assisting them to operate supernaturally. These habits are: *the virtues* which, concurrent with actual grace, enable us to operate supernaturally; and *the gifts* which render us so docile to the action of the Holy Spirit, that guided by a kind of *divine instinct* we are moved and directed by this Divine Spirit.

Inveterate practice of the virtues, of mortification, and of prayer facilitate in our soul the acquisition of docility to the inspirations of the Holy Spirit, and give rise in us to a frequency and intensity in the exercise of the gifts of the Holy Spirit. In the practice of the virtues, grace leaves us active under the influence of prudence, while in the use of the gifts, grace primarily requires docility rather than activity, so that we might be guided and sustained by the Holy Spirit. A mother can avoid the fall of a tender child in two ways: she may teach him to walk, holding his arms so as to guide and support him; or she can pick him up in her arms, thwarting a danger; or she may carry him, because he is tired. So, too, does God deal with our soul. In the exercise of the virtues, leaving the initiative to us, he helps us to work according to the rules of prudence or reason illumined by faith; with the gifts, it is he who commences the work in us, sending us illustrations and inspirations which work in us without our deliberation, requiring, however, our full and willing consent.

Using the examples of the Fathers of the Church, we can say that one who practices virtue, navigates by rowing on his own power. One who is activated by the gifts of the Holy Spirit navigates by sailing, moves more rapidly and relatively without effort, other than docilely following the direction of the wind. One who plays the harp, plucks the strings, and thus is alikened to one who, with order and prudence, practices virtue supernaturally. One who offers the harp to an artist of great renown allows him the freedom to play it magnificently as he pleases, and thus is a likeness to one who, precisely in being docile to the gifts of the Holy Spirit, gives himself to God to be used according to God's good pleasure.

From these concepts, one clearly perceives and better understands what the gifts of the Holy Spirit actually are. Theology defines them thus: *The gifts of the Holy Spirit are supernatural habits which confer on the faculties such docility as to obey promptly the inspirations of grace.* One and the same word – gift – expresses two things: the soul passes under the action of God and receives that action from God's generous liberality as *gift*. The soul, however, is active because it cultivates the gift and desires to do the Divine Will; it is compliant with God and energetic in working, docile to the Love which moves it, and strong in overcoming self so as to follow him without setting up roadblocks.

VII. Action of the Holy Spirit in the Soul: Synthesis

In a materialistic age, and it is necessary to say, in a time of unrestrained sexual license such as that in which we live, it is very difficult to penetrate the soul with some idea of how divine grace and the action of the Holy Spirit work in us. Nonetheless, these concepts and knowledge are very essential for Christian life, for its perfection, and for sanctity. If the soul were to think just this: that the Holy Spirit truly dwells in it, how could the soul possibly yearn for the pleasures of the flesh and commit a sin of impurity? If the soul were to realize that the Holy Spirit is guiding it, how could the soul not hold his hands and allow itself to be directed? For this reason, even at the risk of being redundant, we want to give here a synthesis of all the actions of the Holy Spirit in us, so that the very repetition of concepts makes the truth more evident.

1) The Holy Spirit gives himself to the soul as Author of the supernatural state, without whom, and outside of whom, it is not possible to please God nor to work out one's salvation. This self-communication is necessary, because no man can perform supernatural actions if God does not lift him above all the powers of nature, and by means of that elevation, render him active in living and working in a supernatural way.

To illustrate this by way of analogy, here is what also happens within a purely natural context: A man cannot attain a state beyond that of merely animalistic life without the elevation made possible by education and study. An academic degree raises him above the level of merely material life to that of art and science. He then is no longer a vulgar man who lives solely to eat, drink, and engage in demeaning activities; but he is a scientist who has raised himself to the knowledge of natural truths, and is an artist who discovers his home among the beauty and harmonies of art. The sum total of the knowledge and dispositions which uplifts him, imprints within him a certain permanent character, enabling him to reflect deeply and work nobly.

This character, lifting him to a superior state, gives us some idea of what, in us, is an elevation from the natural to the supernatural state, and of what, in us, is actual grace. The animalistic or carnal man becomes, via this grace, a spiritual man, and he who could not lift himself beyond simple, natural knowledge or the harmonies of created beauty, is now elevated to the plane of supernatural knowledge and the harmonies of eternal beauty. Educational institutions and university study lift a man to a higher state of culture and art. And the Church, through which and in which man lives the life of grace is, as it were, a wonderful institute in which God raises souls to supernatural life.

Such an elevation is the first operation for which the Holy Spirit gives himself to men; and it is realized by means of Baptism or the sacrament of Penance, since by means of these sacraments, the Spirit takes man out of the state of sin, transmits to him sanctifying grace, the supernatural virtues and his gifts; constitutes him a child of God and gives him the strength and power to live in a supernatural way. This communication occurs in all the just: in babies at Baptism, and in penitents with Confession, as soon as, via a true conversion, they abandon sin.

2) The Holy Spirit gives himself to the soul as the Author of supernatural actions. Although man, in fact, acquires supernatural life with this first communication of which we have just spoken, he is not yet capable of performing even one supernatural action by himself without a new influence of the Holy Spirit. Man is like a ship, says St. Basil, which even if perfectly constructed and equipped with all that is necessary for navigation, cannot move without a favorable wind. The influence of the Holy Spirit is so necessary and universal, that no one can do any good without it. St. Cyril of Jerusalem says: *This Consoler sent by God is the director, the teacher, the sanctifier of all. All have need of him: Elijah and Isaiah among men, Gabriel and Michael among the Archangels [Catecheses, 16].*

Machinery is perfect when it is completely mounted and all its parts connected. It represents a wonder of technology and is the complete transformation of prime matter from which it is made. He who sees prime matter in its raw state, finds himself in the presence of unworked mass, jumbled rusting heaps, heavy greenish blocks lying about the earth. This is the natural state of matter. From an unformed and practically useless condition, matter passes to a higher state in the forges, in the electric ovens, under tooling or the power hammer, and while remaining substantially what it was, acquires in its transformation a new entity: it has been worked according to a design precise in each of its parts; it has been structured in view of an end which it must achieve, to be beheld all beautiful in its ordered and harmonious construction. Although complete, it still cannot move itself, nor produce without electric current, nor without some kind of motor, even if only operated by hand.

In an immensely higher sense, the soul in its elevation to the supernatural order by means of habitual grace, is that which is the *prime matter* of this noble transformation. That which is the current or motor for the already completed machine, is the action of the Holy Spirit, an action which actually brings to pass, supernatural actions in the soul. This action is known as the *actual* grace of the Holy Spirit. *Actual,* as the word itself declares, for each act, for every good action which must be accomplished, if only *to pronounce with devotion the name of Jesus,* as St. Paul expressly notes [I Cor 12: 3]. The Holy Spirit enlightens the intellect and forcefully touches the will; the soul is fascinated, feels persuaded, convinced, affected, softened, and passes from capacity to act to acting in fact, pronouncing in loving adoration the name of Jesus.

This influence of the Holy Spirit is so necessary, that no one can do any good without it. It is the wondrous power, the breath, the spirit, the energy which makes possible the harmonies of adoration and of love. Like an immense organ, it intones the praises of God on earth and in eternity, and fills the created spirits and souls with an ineffable joy and an unlimited happiness.[8]

3) *The Holy Spirit gives himself to the soul as Author and Teacher in the way of faith.* His only aim is to lead the soul to holiness. Hence, he begins by prompting it with his holy inspirations to despise the goods of earth, to self-denial, to love of God and of neighbor, and to the exercise of other demanding virtues. The soul exercises itself in these virtues out of love for God and on the principles of faith. Faith increases by means of the seven gifts of the Holy Spirit. This Eternal

---

8 From this simple illustration one can see how much harm is caused by the accursed spirit of naturalism and rationalism, of criticism and foolish scientism which seeps into souls today. The fruit of this spirit is a kind of abhorrence of the supernatural and the tendency to explain everything in terms of reason and natural powers.

Love communicates to the soul a clear, infused light which illuminates the truths of the Faith to it. The soul believes with the simplicity and evidence of one who indeed sees, considerably more than one who sees, because the soul *lives* by faith, savors it and tastes its harmonies, studies its grandeurs in depth, beholds in its light the vanity of earthly things and all the meanness of human reasoning. The soul still remains in the dark; yet the dark is not darkness to it, but rather, the shadows of restful abandonment in God; just as shade, emerging during a day of burning and brilliant sunshine, provides respite.

In the noonday light and in the soft shade of this faith, the Holy Spirit prompts the soul to good, touching and penetrating the heart, making pleasing that which is bitter in the exercise of virtue, and overcoming the pain and resistance of nature. With generous and magnanimous feelings, the Spirit arouses the soul to heroic actions, and responds with miracles to acts of confidence on its part. The soul hopes from God all good, loves him with its whole heart, becomes ever more attentive and docile to the operations of grace, grows in holiness, and can be drawn to the highest forms of contemplation.

WITH A FEW analogies, let us try to deepen these basic concepts, touching the operation of the Holy Spirit in us. A father prepares his son for life in society and in matters of the intellect. By educating him, he corrects and modifies the bad inclinations and disorderly habits of his son, and induces in him inclinations to courtesy, kindness, and generosity which he previously lacked. The son appears a changed person, and even though remaining physically as he was, in reality, he is different. He possesses virtuous habits and inclinations, but based on natural principles: fittingness, modesty, self-esteem, emulation, so as not to be the disgrace of the family, of the name he bears, of the office he occupies.

The *infused* virtues – those conferred by God on the faculties of the soul as supernatural habits, capable of enabling us to gain eternal life – are as it were, the supernatural education which the Lord himself gives us; are *principles of action,* as theology defines them, *which God inserts in us to serve the soul as supernatural powers, making it easy for the soul to perform meritorious acts.*

Natural virtues are acquired with the repetition of the same acts, under the spur and vigilance of the educator; the supernatural virtues come from God who infuses them into the soul together with habitual grace. It is logical that God, in elevating us to the supernatural order with habitual grace, should give us those habits and those powers which are proportioned to that order, we might say, precisely so that we might not be a disgrace in the higher order. He who confers on a plebian a title of nobility takes care that the recipient learns how to speak well and to act courteously, so as not to cut a shameful figure. *The infused virtues* give us a *facility* to perform acts of virtue promptly and joyfully; they give us *the power* to perform meritorious acts, and a certain *inclination* to perform them. By repeating acts of these virtues, they become ever more easy, not merely tending to the greater good as in the natural virtues, but to the friendship and glory of One and Triune God.

The virtues increase in the measure in which habitual grace increases in us. God produces this increase when we receive the Sacraments, perform good works, and pray. Thus one comes, as St. Thomas says, to a more perfect and more active possession of the virtues, and these sink their roots in us more deeply, becoming more stable and fruitful. Venial sins block the exercise of the virtues; mortal sins undermine the foundations of those linked to charity. Faith and hope remain in the sinner, but in a state of inactivity, as a kind of anchor of salvation, provided one not sin directly against these two virtues.

From these concepts and those given previously, one sees clearly how the virtues differ from the gifts of the Holy Spirit.

The virtues are powers directly *active*, inclining us to act according to the nature of our faculties, such that with the help of the graces conferred on us, we probe, reason, and work in the same way as in the case of activity in the purely natural order, even if acting supernaturally.

One who paints with brushes that serve to produce masterpieces of art, holds and moves them in the same way as one who traces simple colored lines with them at the base of a gate. The portrait painter is an artist who lives in the higher order of art; the house painter is a manual laborer who applies a simple color with a certain symmetry.

The gifts of the Holy Spirit give the soul the *docility* to follow the promptings of actual grace, a grace which sets our faculties in motion without, however, depriving them of their freedom. In the virtues, we direct ourselves according to principles and rules *of supernatural prudence*, in such wise that we might reflect, consult, deliberate, choose, etc. Under the influence of the gifts, we let ourselves be guided instead by *a divine motion* which immediately, and without our reflection, makes us hasten to do this or that thing.

The Gifts of the Holy Spirit[9]

9   The theological explanation of the gifts by St. Thomas (cf. *Summa Theologica*, IIa IIae) is found in the context of an exposition of the virtues. One may usefully compare this with a complementary exposition of virtues, gifts and beatitudes by St. Bonaventure, in summary form in his *Breviloquium*, part 5, ch. 4–6. In both Saints the discussion follows upon a discussion of grace, with particular stress on the gift of the Holy Spirit in St. Bonaventure consequent on the redemptive sacrifice of Jesus. [Tr. note]

CஜBஜ

I. Necessity and Manner of Cultivating the Gifts of the Holy Spirit in Us

No field can produce fruit if not cultivated, and no thing or precious object can be preserved without maintenance. A house without maintenance decays little by little and falls into ruin. The wallpaper drops from the walls, the walls crumble, the bricks loosen, the doors jam, etc. Supernatural goods also need to be cultivated and stand in need of a certain spiritual maintenance as well. This cultivation is at the same time a disposition for receiving them properly and a means for increasing them and making them bear fruit in us.

To attain this sublime goal, before any other consideration it is necessary to exercise the moral virtues. To acquire, in fact, the divine docility which the gifts confer, it is necessary above all to have brought passions and vices under control via habits of prudence, humility, obedience, delicacy, chastity, and in general all the virtues opposed to the seven capital sins.

How can one perceive, docilely accept, and follow the inspirations of grace, when one's soul is agitated by the imprudence of the flesh which makes it cowardly, opportunistic and two-faced; when it is bloated with pride and restlessness due to lack of moral character driven by anger and more so by lust? From this simple reflection, one sees immediately the true cause of the sterility of the grace of the Holy Spirit in so many souls who receive Confirmation, preceded by a hasty Confession and without true dispositions of repentance and emendation; who receive the Sacrament with vices of every kind and after Confirmation, continue to indulge the same vices to which they are slaves. A piece of rusted equipment with jammed mechanisms and switches, receives a current that should set it into motion, yet the charge simply vibrates in the machinery, as in a team set to run a race. For all intended purposes, the machine remains without power; it is neither docile nor responsive to the impulse of the current that should activate it. If, however, the resisting parts are cleaned and oiled, it will operate with ease, because only under such conditions, may it be described as docile.

There are souls given to the spiritual life, who believe they can elevate themselves by means of a superficial devotion, and often delude themselves in thinking they have reached contemplation and holiness, without realizing they have retained all their vices. After years of spiritual life, they find themselves still lacking in virtue, impatient, irritable and proud, little experienced, and anything but docile to the Holy Spirit. They are like clocks, polished and adorned with external ornaments, but whose machinery is clogged with rust. In some small way, they are pleasant in appearance; but unresponsive to the impulse of the cord, they fail to sound the hours of God. The cord remains in its case, tightly wound and ready to spring, but in fact unable to unwind.

The gifts of the Holy Spirit are also cultivated by combating the spirit of the world, which is diametrically opposed to that of God. The *natural* man, or as St. Paul calls him, the *animalistic* man, does not accept the things of the spirit of God; for him these are foolishness and he cannot grasp them. To combat the spirit of the world, one must flee all those habits of modern life which make that spirit flourish within us: theatre, cinema, frivolous or perverse printed material, dangerous friendships, worldly conversation. And it is necessary to read the Gospel, the Scriptures, the lives of the saints, and all that might enlighten the soul in the ways of God.

With the elimination of the spirit of the world, it is necessary to have recourse to those positive and direct means of placing oneself under the action of the Holy Spirit. First of all, it is necessary to cultivate *interior recollection* and the habit of thinking of God often. Then the Holy Spirit speaks to the heart, giving the soul light, strength, and consolation. It is necessary to habituate oneself to make sacrifices for the Lord and, therefore, to exercise oneself in self-denial and in penance. It is necessary to pray and often invoke the Holy Spirit with great, filial confidence – in union with Jesus Christ who promised to send us His Spirit, and in union with Mary Most Holy – as the Apostles did in the Cenacle. The Church has most beautiful prayers to the Holy Spirit, such as the hymn *Veni, Creator Spiritus* [Come, Creator Spirit], the sequence *Veni, Sancte Spiritus* [Come, Holy Spirit], the collect *Uri igne Sancti Spiritus* [Burn with the fire of the Holy Spirit], with secret and post-communion [of the votive Mass of the Holy Spirit].

II. Gifts of Nature and Gifts of the Holy Spirit

What is a gift of nature, for example, the gift of painting, or music, or art, or of poetry? We might repeat here, in another context, the definition we have already given of the gifts of the Holy Spirit: *It is a natural habit, a fixed inclination, which confers a facility in performing some action and work of a higher order in the general field of human activity.*

The gift of nature is also a gift from God, and the Lord gives such a gift so that an individual might carry out a specific mission for the good of all mankind, or more simply, for the adornment and dignity of mankind. That there should be a capable painter like Raphael, for example, is not a necessity for mankind strictly speaking, but is an aspect of that dignity which ennobles our race, and can also produce some good, raising souls from a base, materialistic way of life to a certain level of spirituality.

Art is truly like a first dim and tenuous ray of that spirituality which finds its maximal splendor in holiness. By art, we mean true art, understood in its noble form, not in those miserable examples which are passed off as art and which, in fact, are the caricature and degradation of true art. Art thus conceived, does not elevate the spirit, but abases and renders it ugly. True art glorifies the works of God, attracts, moves the soul, and gently leads it to meditate.

It is by way of synthesis a book of meditations, not expressed verbally, but in color, with bas-reliefs, with a gesture fixing the eye of the soul on a truth, a thought, a sentiment and thus refines it. False art, immoral and impure, is the degradation of a thought and of an affection in the indulgence of impurity. Hence, the so-called art for art's sake [*ars gratia artis*], amoral or immoral, is an enormous blunder, and anyone promoting this is either not a true artist, or is one of those pseudo-philosophic sophists, who only cares for the form, and not the substance of art.

The gifts of nature enable us to better understand, by way of analogy, the gifts of the Holy Spirit: *supernatural habits infused by the Holy Spirit to give the human soul a higher kind of activity, and give the faculties of the soul itself, such docility as to promptly obey the inspirations of grace.* These inspirations or promptings are the ideals or exemplars of the divine art of sanctification; and the gift is the inclination of the soul to function with ease in a holy way on a higher plane. To make ourselves even clearer we might say as is said today of gifts of nature, it is… *the flair* for a higher and supernatural activity. The gift of *Wisdom, for example, makes us discern and assess God and the things of God in their highest principles, and makes us taste them.* This gift is the sublime philosophy of the supernatural; and as a true philosopher, a born philosopher, one who has the *philosophical flair,* intuits natural truths in their principles and in their causes with ease, and discusses these with pleasure because they delight him; so one who has the gift of Wisdom intuits supernatural truths, discusses them or meditates on them with joyous exultation, and easily grasps the enlightenment which the Holy Spirit grants him, living the Faith in a grand interior light.

That which in the philosopher is the depth of human thought, is in the soul in possession of the gift of Wisdom, the deepened appreciation of the grandeur of God and of things divine. This enables such a person to know God with that perfection which is possible to him within the limits of our present life, a life not of eternal glory, but of exile. From the considerations on each of the gifts of the Holy Spirit, one will grasp still better this concept which gives us a clearer idea of those ineffable gifts.

With the gifts of nature, it is not enough to possess the easy and spontaneous inclination in a particular faculty or activity. It is necessary to *cultivate that inclination,* and therefore to apply oneself, to exercise oneself, to put oneself under the guidance of a master. With the gifts of the Holy Spirit a cultivation is also required, as we have already said; and this cultivation in not only a general one, applicable to all the gifts, but is particular for each one, as we shall see. This assiduous cultivation places the soul ever more in the condition of docility to the promptings of the Holy Spirit, and raises it, little by little, to the heights of perfection and holiness.

III. Gifts of the Holy Spirit: Number – Reason for This Number – Their Classification

The gifts of the Holy Spirit are enumerated by the Prophet Isaiah. Announcing the future Redeemer as Son of Mary Most Holy, a descendant of the family of David, Isaiah prophetically proclaims that on Him shall rest the Spirit of the Lord. In fact that Spirit descended on Jesus when He asked to be baptized by St. John the Baptist.

Here are the words of the Prophet, and here is the enumeration which he makes of the gifts of the Holy Spirit: *There shall come forth a rod out of the root of Jesse* [Jesse is a form of Isai, the name of the father of David], *and a flower shall rise up out of his root* [the rod and the flower was Jesus Christ, Son of Mary Most Holy]. *And the Spirit of the Lord shall rest upon Him: the spirit of wisdom and of understanding, the spirit of counsel and of fortitude, the spirit of knowledge and of godliness* [piety]. *And he shall be filled with the spirit of the fear of the Lord* [11: 1–3].

As one can see, there are seven gifts of the Holy Spirit; the very same which with greater or less intensity descend on the Christian soul when it receives the Holy Spirit in Confirmation. Becoming a member of Jesus Christ through Baptism, the soul participates in the very gifts which He possesses in their wonderful fullness.

One may ask: Why are there seven gifts? There are seven, because these correspond to the seven principal needs and activities of the supernatural life of the soul. There are seven, because they are opposed to the seven capital sins; because being seven states of life, they are opposed to seven states of death. The soul which is the living temple of the Most Holy Trinity has, so to say, lighted in itself a seven-branched candlestick, has in its powers an adoring hierarchy, like that of the seven celestial spirits, who stand before the throne of God.

The soul, in fact, has need to know how to learn about and taste divine things, in order to be attracted to and love the Lord more, and behold the gift of *Wisdom* which enables it to perceive and savor the revealed truths. It has need of deepening and penetrating them in order to find hidden treasures and mysterious harmonies – and behold the gift of *Understanding*. It has need of applying these to each exigency of the interior life – and behold the gift of *Counsel*. It has need to profess, in high profile and against all opposition, the truths which it knows – and behold the gift of *Fortitude*.

Living on earth, the soul requires that created things not be an obstacle to those divine and eternal; rather it is necessary that by the former, the soul be lifted up to God, considering them in their relation with God – and behold the gift of *Knowledge*. The soul has need like a daughter to open herself tenderly to God and rejoice in glorifying him in all things – and behold the gift of *Godliness*. Loving God with holy intimacy and familiarity, the soul must not become forgetful of his majesty, nor his justice – and behold the gift of the *Fear of the Lord*.

Fearing God, the soul humbles herself in his sight, and conquers *pride* which flares up against him. Opening herself to God as a daughter, the soul regards him as supreme good and conquers *avarice* which, in disorderly fashion, attracts her to the goods of earth. Lifting herself up from the things of earth to those of Heaven, the soul abhors the disorder of *lust* which immerses one in the most putrid mire of earthly things. The soul conquers *anger* with fortitude of the spirit. She conquers *gluttony* tasting heavenly things, in not taking as goal of life, immoderate satisfaction from eating and drinking. The soul conquers *envy*, considering the image of God in one's neighbor, and loving in God the bestowal of goods of nature and of grace. The soul conquers *boredom*, because knowing God, she senses the ardor of her own heart and feels the need to glorify, to love, to pray, and to converse with him.

By means of the seven gifts of the Holy Spirit, the soul is like a candlestick with seven branches and seven lamps which burn before the Most Holy Trinity dwelling in it. The lamp is a light shining in the darkness which makes possible the vision of objects. And the gifts of the Holy Spirit are supernatural lights of the soul which enlighten its powers, and so render them docile to the promptings of grace and to the interior awareness of God's designs.

In accord with the particular mission God assigns to each soul, one gift rather than another will be more in evidence. And because the powers of the soul do not all have the same perfection, the gifts of the Holy Spirit can, therefore, be arranged in descending scale of perfection, beginning with the

gift of Wisdom which is the highest in perfection, concluding
with Fear at the bottom of the scale. It is rare, in fact, that with
the fear of God, there is perfect love in the soul; not because
the gift is deficient, but because of defects in the soul. To weak
souls, still bound to earth, even if the seven gifts were poured
out on them in Confirmation, the Holy Spirit gives a larger
share in the Fear of the Lord, so that from this gift they might
be lifted up to a fuller knowledge and love of God.

IF THE FACULTIES on which the gifts of the Holy Spirit
act, are taken into consideration, the gifts may be classified as
intellectual and *affective* or of the will. The first illumine the
intellect, and are *knowledge, understanding, wisdom* and *counsel*.
The second strengthen the will, and are *fortitude, godliness* and
fear of the Lord. Among the intellectual gifts three specially
produce infused contemplation: *knowledge, understanding* and
wisdom. These, in fact, elevate the soul to God in the luminous
consideration of his grandeur, or in loving admiration of his
works. The other gifts are said to be *active*, because they move
the soul to work for God or to arouse itself in his love.

The gifts perfect the virtues and render them heroic,
prodding the soul to those acts which are in need of a special
power to be performed. With his grace, the Holy Spirit makes
the soul virtuous; with the gifts, he makes it heroic. The gift
of *Wisdom* perfects the virtue of *charity* or love for God and
reflexively love for neighbor. The gifts of *Understanding* and
of *Knowledge* perfect the virtue of *faith*. The gift of *Counsel*
perfects the virtue of *prudence*. The gift of *Fortitude* perfects
the virtue of *fortitude*. The gift of *Godliness* perfects the virtue
of *religion*, and the annexed virtue, *justice*, because there is
no greater justice than to honor God in himself and in one's
neighbor, who is his image. The gift of *Fear of the Lord* perfects
the virtues of *hope* and of *temperance*. Thus, the gifts of the
Holy Spirit perfect the three fundamental virtues known as
theological, because their object is God: *faith, hope* and *charity*,
and the four virtues known as cardinal, because they are the

hinges [in Latin *cardinalis* means hinging]: *justice, prudence, fortitude* and *temperance.*

From the exposition and explanation of the individual gifts of the Holy Spirit, this relation between gifts and virtues will become much clearer. To say this with the help of an example: the virtue is like machinery *in a series,* as they say: good and complete in its parts, but not capable of manufacturing delicately finished products. The gift is like a precision machine which produces the objects manufactured by serial machinery fully refined and exquisitely beautiful. An ordinary watch, for example, tells time, and therefore, serves its intended purpose; an *Omega* however, indicates the hours with greater precision, counting the seconds. An average automobile speeds up, slows down, stops, etc., responding to its various operational functions, although somewhat roughly perhaps. A luxury auto, on the other hand, designed to optimal perfection, operating smoothly or docilely, without the slightest jolt or noise, will react instantaneously to the driver's mode of application.[10]

IV. Gifts of the Holy Spirit in Particular – The Gift of Wisdom

In considering the gifts of the Holy Spirit in particular, we follow the order in which they appear in Isaiah and in the Church. We may note in general that, since the gifts are *supernatural habits* which prepare new advances in the ways of perfection, and since *they confer on the faculties docility to obey the promptings of grace,* they presuppose the exercise of the virtues which the gifts themselves perfect. For what is not even rough-hewn, logically cannot be finished.

The lack of virtue, therefore, so common in souls, is the reason for their supernatural sterility, even though they have been confirmed. Sadly enough, it is very rare to find souls in whom the gifts of the Holy Spirit shine forth, or in whom at

---

10 Automobile technology as we know it today, is much more refined, even in less expensive models [Tr. note].

least a few flourish. The Holy Spirit descends in them when they receive the Sacrament of Confirmation and pours forth his gifts. But these remain in them as a divine power marginally attached to their faculties, and practically do not become *habits* until they are cultivated; they do not pass from the potentiality to the actuality of a perfect virtue, until the souls are prodded to exercise the basic virtues which the gifts perfect.

The gifts, therefore, are bestowed gratuitously, but require preparation and correspondence for the cultivation of the gifts themselves. Hence, in treating the individual gifts, we have added to each set of considerations a practical method for cultivating that gift. We repeat, because it is of the greatest importance: we receive the gifts of the Holy Spirit in conjunction with the state of grace; but at that point, they are nothing but simple, supernatural powers. Even a baby who receives life receives natural powers, but these remain in need of development.

The gifts of the Holy Spirit begin to be developed in the soul under the influence of actual grace, and so set in motion the entire supernatural organism. These actual graces influence, at least *latently*, every meritorious act. The full exercise of the gifts is not realized except with the full exercise of the virtues, because only then is the soul fully attentive to God, fully docile under his prompting, and able to be spurred to heroic acts, which are the fully mature fruit of the gift or gifts which the soul has received.

THE GIFT OF Wisdom, which we must now treat in particular, is the first of three gifts called *intellectual*, gifts which concur most directly in the contemplation of God and of things divine, namely *wisdom, understanding* and *knowledge*. All three have this in common: that they give an *experiential* or quasi-experiential knowledge of divine truths (or of truths which lead to God), because they make us know, not by way of discursive reasoning, but by means of a superior light which makes us understand as though we had experienced the truth. This light, communicated to us by the Holy Spirit, is certainly the light of Faith, but more active and more illuminating than is habitually the case. This light gives us a kind of intuition of these truths, similar to that of the first principles of a science, evident as axioms, e.g., 4+4 equals 8.

The gift of Wisdom is a gift which perfects the virtue of charity, and is at once found in both the intellect and the will, because it pours light and love into the soul. It is the most excellent of the gifts that recapitulates all the others, just as charity includes all the virtues. It is defined thus: *A gift which in perfecting the virtue of charity, makes us discern and assess God and the things of God in their highest principles and makes us taste them.* It communicates to man *a light* which makes him know God with that perfection which is possible to him. It communicates *a love* whereby man loves and understands God in a most tender fashion. It bestows an interior change whereby man comes to be wholly transformed into God. This gift is the goal of all the others; it renders us perfectly happy in this world and intimately unites us to God, because it makes us know him in an ineffable way.

The soul who receives this light is like a blind man who receives sight as an adult. What did this man think of the world before receiving sight? He believed in the existence of the sun, the moon, and the stars; he believed there were trees, flowers, fruits, birds, and animals; he believed in the mountains, the hills, the sea, and in all else of which he might be told, or of which he might have a certain experience by touch. But none of these things could excite in him that joy and that desire which are naturally aroused in those who contemplate them. In this profound obscurity – which could also account for his having distorted ideas of things whose existence he accepted, on the basis of what others told him of them – he is suddenly gifted with sight; he sees the sun, the mountains, the sea, the plants, the flowers, and becomes ecstatic in this vision from which he does not want to separate himself for the sake of the joy and satisfaction it produces in him. So it is with the soul upon receiving the gift of Wisdom. First, with the light of faith, the soul believes that God is infinite, the inexhaustible source of all perfections, infinitely powerful, wise, loving, and good; but the light of the soul's faith being weak, can neither excite in the soul much love for God, nor much contentment. After having received the light of the gift of Wisdom, what a change occurs in the soul in an instant! The divine perfections are shown to the soul in great splendor; the soul lives of them, exults in them, is afire with love, and utterly beside itself, immersed in that divine sea.

And not only does the soul know God in a most clear fashion such as to make evident and profoundly convincing the faith which it has in him, but it tastes the magnificent grandeur, and in recollection and profound exultation, rejoices in it. St. Bernard for this reason calls the gift of *Wisdom a savory knowledge of things divine.* And St. Bonaventure adds that *it is one thing to know that honey is sweet, and another thing to eat it and really taste its sweetness.*

A soul which has the light of Faith believes and knows that God is infinitely sweet, but does not experience the taste of this sweetness. When, however, that soul receives the gift of Wisdom, not only does it know in a brilliant light that what it believes is true, but tastes this sweetness, and the soul's whole heart is filled and replete with it. For this reason, the saints who were inundated with this gift, found their every joy and contentment in prayer, and knew not how to withdraw themselves from it. St. Francis Borgia used to say to those who begged him to bring his prayer to an end: *O my dear brother, let me taste my joy for a quarter hour!*

The soul is, in a sense, wrapped in a hidden ray of interior sun which provides it with light in its darkness and warmth in its exposure, experiencing a joy and a peace that fills it with happiness. *The light* for the soul is a quiet evidence, giving it sweet repose in the truth of Faith which sees a vast, divine synthesis in the highest causes and their unity; *the warmth* is a profound love, a *supernatural taste* that works on the will, making it savor the things of God by means of a kind of hidden connaturality or harmony. These things are true, lovely, sweet; the soul feels God, sees him, tastes him; it is convinced of these truths, exults in them, enjoys them; and this is innate for the soul because it has neither the shadow of a doubt nor clouded diffidence. Its certainty is love; its love is replete; the soul's abundance effects an overflow of admiration for all that is harmoniously beautiful in the Faith, and expands its confidence in God to whom it feels most akin in that harmony.

Hence, the gift of Wisdom communicates to the soul a love whereby it understands and loves God in a most tender way. This love is what we commonly call *fervor*. It is not a love of esteem, possible to be had with the simple light of faith, but it is a love which penetrates the entire soul and there imparts a palpable sweetness; it is a flame which ignites the heart and makes it overflow in God. In this state few affections are formed, few sighs, few words; the heart burns tranquilly; all its powers are united in God, and the soul in profound peace accepts it and does naught else but love and burn.

This love is constant in the soul, and transforms it entirely in God. The Holy Spirit represses and annihilates in the soul inclinations, affections and natural desires, and then there exists no other love in the soul but love for God and for neighbor, out of love for God. The soul's only joy is the glory of God; It has no other sadness but that caused by sin and the loss of souls, no other desire but to love God more fervently, no other yearning but to work and suffer for him still more.

The Holy Spirit gives tranquility and silence to all the powers of the soul, and governs it himself. He directs the soul's interior life; he gives himself to its memory, in such wise that the soul remembers God always; he gives himself to the soul's intellect, that it sees in God ever new wonders and perfections;

he gives himself to the soul's will that it burns always with new flames. The Holy Spirit also directs the exterior life of the soul, and via an internal light, makes the soul know that which it must do in order to please God in everything, in such wise that its life becomes all holy and perfect.

From what has been said, we may summarily deduce: *1)* That as distinct from the gift of Understanding which makes us know divine truths in themselves and in their mutual relations, the gift of Wisdom makes us know them in their highest causes, and makes us taste and enjoy them. *2)* The gift of Wisdom, in addition to the increase of charity which it produces in the soul, perfects all the other virtues; it therefore renders faith *unshakable* by means of the quasi-experiential knowledge it gives of revealed truths. He who has ever savored at length, the delights of Communion or the sweet intimacy of visits to Jesus in the Blessed Sacrament, cannot doubt His real presence under the Eucharistic species.

By means of the gift of Wisdom, the soul enjoys a most certain faith. Such faith strengthens *hope* in the soul, because the soul knows it is tending to God and must possess God eternally. On earth the soul lives and tastes union with Jesus, and hopes to unite itself to Him eternally, together with the saints who reign with Him. Inflamed as it is by love, the soul desires nothing else but to resemble Jesus and please Him, and hence to feel in itself, in virtue of the very gift of Wisdom, a greater spur and strength to practice the moral virtues. After savoring the delights of the love of God, those of earth no longer meet the soul's tastes or attractions, for the soul loves the Cross, mortification, humility, gentleness, patience and all the other virtues.

V. Means for Cultivating the Gift of Wisdom

That which produces the gift of Wisdom in the soul is neither active nor fully efficient in every creature receiving that gift, because this requires preparation on the part of the soul to receive it well, and correspondence in its cultivation afterwards. Were the gift to effect in a single moment all the effects it is capable of producing, every confirmed soul would automatically be a saint. It is not enough to possess the natural gift of art to be a perfect artist; the habitual inclination to use that gift and the very facility the artist experiences in using it, far from making him lazy, engage him with still greater zest and joy to experience it more; and therefore, that zest and joy arouse in him the need to cultivate it. So, too, with the gifts of the Holy Spirit and in particular the gift of Wisdom; the soul must correspond with it and nurture it.

A crane, lifting heavy materials next to a warehouse entrance, is like a giant hand reaching out toward tons of massive cargo and raising it up as though mere wisps of straw. In the crane's cabin, however, there is an operator who must maneuver and set the crane in motion with a current of electricity. Without that operator, that strategy, and that maneuver, the crane still retains great power, but in reality, it fails to be energized. With its power set in motion, the crane facilitates work in gigantic enterprises, in the face of which even the Cyclops would be useless. The operator, however, must first prepare by learning its functions and, then must in fact, fully engage its power.

When Jesus Christ wished to send the Holy Spirit on the Apostles, He made them gather in prayer in the Cenacle, together with Mary Most Holy, full of grace, so that they might prepare and receive assistance from the Immaculate Virgin, for the great gift which would transform them into new creatures.

After having received the ineffable gifts, the Apostles immediately emerged from the Cenacle to fulfill their mission. They rendered active the gifts they had just received; they corresponded with them and cultivated them interiorly by living lives entirely holy and immaculate. The Christian soul cannot conduct itself differently if it does not want to receive in vain, the immense riches and incomparable power of the gift of the Holy Spirit. If one recalls that Jesus Christ gave the Eucharist to the Apostles without any proximate preparation, but did not send the Holy Spirit without *imposing* upon them a time of reflection and prayer, the soul will understand why it has the precise duty of preparing with great diligence for reception of the Holy Spirit; and upon having accepted him, to match that gift with intense, personal correspondence.

With particular regard to the gift of Wisdom, the soul must ardently desire it and implore it with manifold prayers. These prayers will draw him upon the soul, and when it has received the Holy Spirit, will make this gift develop and grow interiorly. For invoking the Holy Spirit, the most beautiful prayers are those which the Church uses, namely, the *Veni, Creator Spiritus* [Come, Creator Spirit], the *Veni, Sancte Spiritus, et emitte caelitus lucis tuae radium* [Come, Holy Spirit, and send forth from heaven a ray of thy light] and *Veni, Sancte Spiritus, reple tuorum corda fidelium* [Come, Holy Spirit, fill the hearts of thy faithful].

IN ORDER TO be effective, some medications require abstinence from certain kinds of foods; and some foods can even convert medicine into poison. Acidulous fruits such as lemons, change [chamomile] into [sublimate] thus producing a poisonous substance. If the gift of Wisdom makes us *taste* the things of God, it is obvious that the soul cannot simultaneously assimilate the poison of worldly things, or even worse, the perverted taste of impurity. It is, therefore, exceedingly dangerous to read books, reviews, or frivolous, evil publications; to relax with degrading entertainment, or to socialize in worldly circles. How can the sun shine in a place filled with thick, unctuous, noxious smoke, or in a fogbound swamp? To preserve a taste for music, it is essential to listen to classical compositions and always avoid whatever might hinder its refinement. To acquire a taste for the things of God, it is necessary to become familiar with them through holy reading, meditation, and interior recollection.

To cultivate the gift of Wisdom, then, it is necessary to have a pure heart, for as Jesus says: *Blessed are the pure of heart, for they shall see God.* The great lens through which one may distinctly view the magnificence of God is precisely purity of the soul, of the heart, and of the senses. At the present time, the world is submerged in impurity, and this impurity flows back upon the soul like a putrid torrent, through the five bodily senses, which explains why there is such impoverishment in the gifts of the Holy Spirit, particularly in the gift of Wisdom.

The eyes focus on nothing but shameful nudity; the ears hear nothing other than obscene conversations; the taste buds are tantalized by food and drink that arouse unchaste sensations; the sense of smell is provoked by sensuous fragrances; feelings are stimulated by continuous, dangerous touches. For these reasons, the flavor for things divine has been completely lost, and every day, the world becomes increasingly torpid.

Let us, then, incessantly beg the Lord to substitute for the senses of the body those of the soul; let us pray in the beautiful words of St. Augustine: *What do I love, O God, when I love thee?... I love a certain light, a certain voice, a certain odor, a certain food, a certain embrace when I love my God, light, voice, odor, food, embrace at the inmost of my consciousness where shines splendidly on my soul what space does not contain, where sounds what time does not transmit, where are fragrant odors which the wind does not dispel, where one savors what is not consumed in being eaten, where one embraces what containment does not render unpalatable. This is what I love when I love my God!* [*Confessions*, Book 10, ch. 7]. O how far we are from divine love and from the taste of this love when we live in impurity!

VI. Gift of Understanding and How to Cultivate It

The gift of Understanding is defined thus: *A gift which under the enlightening action of the Holy Spirit gives us a penetrating intuition into revealed truths, without however revealing the mystery.* The object of this gift is the ensemble of all the revealed truths, which the light of the Holy Spirit makes us see in a single, profound glance; making us penetrate its intimate significance, even though remaining in the context of the mysterious darkness of Faith; and making us perceive the credibility and harmony of this Faith in relation to what is noblest in human reason.

This gift, as St. Thomas teaches [*Summa*, II–II, q. 8, a. 1], makes us penetrate into the very heart of revealed truths in six different ways: *1)* It uncovers for us the substance hidden beneath the accidents, e.g., Jesus under the Eucharistic species. The soul notices the real presence of Jesus, even though not seeing Him, and is most certain that He is there, because the soul has a profound intuition of love. *2)* It explains to us the meaning of the words, hidden under the literal sense of Scripture, as Jesus did for the disciples of Emmaus, revealing to them the meaning of the prophecies in His regard. *3)* It manifests the hidden significance of the sensible signs of the Sacraments, not only with an intellectual intuition, but by making them vital in the soul which intuits that significance. Thus, St. Paul [Rom 6: 3–5] shows us how Baptism by immersion is the symbol of our death to sin, of our spiritual burial and resurrection together with Jesus Christ. *4)* It makes us understand spiritual realities under a phenomenological form in which they appear, e.g., in the worker of Nazareth, the Creator of the world. *5)* It shows us the effects as contained in their cause, e.g., in the Blood of Jesus shed on Calvary, the purification of our soul, and our reconciliation with God; in the wounded side of Jesus, the birth of the Church, and the Sacraments. *6)* It makes us see the cause in the effects, e.g., the action of Providence in the external events of life.

The gift of Understanding shows us revealed truth in such light so as to reassure us in the Faith, and gives to one who must explain the truths of Faith the ability to make them more intelligible via analogies and examples. It is, as it were, a light which makes us see the truths of Faith in their reality, convincing us of them without need of argumentation. The simple light of Faith is like the dim light of a candle which shows us the beauty of a portrait, but with difficulty in appreciating the various details. The light of Understanding is like a ray of living sunshine, enlivening the colors, to the extent that what at first impression seemed a dark spot, appears in sunlight as a lovely blue mantle, etc. He who examines the portrait in the dim light of a lamp, must study each detail to appreciate the full beauty; who examines it in the splendor of sunlight, has need only to see it with a single glance of the eye.

That secure glance of the eye by which the soul sees the mysteries of Faith as a whole, solidifies that very Faith in the soul so convincingly, that it speaks of these mysteries confidently, and is ready to lay down its life to defend the truth. The soul lives of this truth, and living it – loves it – to such a degree that the soul has no other desire than to go to Heaven to enjoy it; and so long as it lives a pilgrim on earth, is all tenderness for God, for Jesus Christ, for the Holy Spirit, and cannot hear these names without being moved and aroused to tender affections.

To cultivate in the soul the gift of Understanding, a living, simple faith is necessary, one which humbly implores of God the light to understand the revealed truths better. *"I praise Thee, Father, Lord of heaven and earth, because Thou didst hide these things from the wise and prudent and didst reveal them to the little ones"* [Mt 11: 25]. To enjoy, therefore, such enduring light, brightly illuminating revealed truths, one must become humble and little. The examples and similarities communicated by the Holy Spirit to the soul as harmonious parts of a single scene, reassure the soul of the Faith. They are an integral aspect of that state of simplicity and humility which is the preparation for, and we would say, the natural environment of this gift of God. On this terrain, the gift of Understanding prospers. This humble, simple glimpse into the grandeur of the supernatural is of such depth that in some way, as St. Thomas says, it makes us see God even in this life, when we are supported by the gift of Understanding.

In this gift, the soul possesses a kind of miraculous telescope for looking into the depths of Heaven; and just as the telescope makes a far distant star visible, although that star remains but a luminous point in the mirror reflecting it, so the gift of the Holy Spirit shows the revealed truths, although leaving them as mysteries. These are still stars which remain points in the mirror, yet their truth and their harmony are fully before the soul, just as the spectacle of distant stars is complete and wonderful before the eye of the astronomer.

Cultivation of the gift of Understanding also requires meditation on these mysteries as a preparation for a more vital grasp of the mysteries of Faith. The soul cannot insist on remaining inactive, or worse distracted by or dissipated in earthly affairs, and still benefit from the gift of the Holy Spirit. The soul must apply itself to meditating on the mysteries, seeking to grasp their meaning, their depth and their analogy with reason. This meditation must be conducted in profound humility, more with the heart than with the mind, more by living the mysteries of Faith than in presuming to examine them critically.

In such humble and affective meditation, the light of the gift of Understanding, like a lamp of living light shining in the obscurity of night, performs its function. Thus, for example, by meditating on the mystery of the Incarnation, and on the glory which the Word become man gives to the Father, the soul better understands that the Incarnate Word is the substantial glory of the Father in the Most Holy Trinity [cf. Heb 1:3]; and grasps in ever greater depth, the mystery of His union with human nature and His redemptive work, a work entirely consisting in a glorification of the Father in souls and in the life of the Catholic Church. A soul who does not meditate, does not activate the gift of Understanding within itself; just as someone who does not study neither exercises nor activates his own intelligence and is unable to enter in depth into the books lying open on a desk, which he perhaps may read, although distractedly at best.

COME, O HOLY Spirit, strengthen my impoverished understanding with thy light; make me grasp the truths of Faith and live them. Come, that my soul, inebriated by light, might enjoy control of my body and feel the need to live blessedly in the truth! Come, enlighten me, that I might discover the ugliness of error, the false arguments of heretics; the foolishness of the impious; and so flee the entrapments of a perverse media to destroy my faith. Come, enlighten me with the light of the saints, that I might live in the knowledge and the love of God: *Veni, Sancte Spiritus!*

VII. Gift of Counsel: Its Nature – Object – Effects – Necessity – Cultivation

The gift of Counsel *perfects the virtue of prudence, enabling it to discern promptly and surely, by means of a kind of supernatural intuition, what is most fitting especially in difficult cases*, this in view of eternal life. With the virtue of prudence we reflect and unfailingly search out the better means for achieving some goal, profiting from past experiences, studying the circumstances of a present affair to be dealt with, so as to adopt a wise solution. With the gift of Counsel comes the Holy Spirit who speaks to the heart, and makes us understand in an instant, what we must do.

For example, the glorious martyrs of all times, according to the promise of Jesus [cf. 12: 11–12], do not respond to tyrants with replies carefully calculated according to the dictates of human prudence, but follow the interior impulses of the Holy

Spirit experienced in their moment of risk. St. Peter, arrested by the Sanhedrin after Pentecost, was given the order not to preach Jesus Christ any longer, but he replied immediately through an evident prompting of the Holy Spirit: *We must obey God rather than men* [Acts 5: 29]. Human prudence would have suggested not to compromise oneself; the Counsel of the Holy Spirit, by contrast, suggested a frank response so as not to deny or betray the mission received from the Lord.

The proper object of the gift of Counsel is the good direction of particular actions. The lights of the Holy Spirit show us what we must do at any time, place or circumstance in which we find ourselves; and if we are charged with the guidance of others, suggests to us the practical way in which we must conduct ourselves.

With the gift of Counsel, the Christian soul has sure discernment of the means to adopt, in order to succeed in an important matter; the soul sees the right way to follow, and walks it fearlessly, however difficult, harsh, and repulsive it might be, knowing how to await the propitious hour of God, and not anticipate events without due consideration. The absence of this gift leaves us confused in our planning, precipitous in our proposals, imprudent in our speech, and rash in our undertakings.

The effects of the gift of Counsel are multiple for the soul, and are reflected in its activities and proposals. This gift, at the interior of the soul, makes it *distinguish between the promptings of grace and those of nature, and repress and control the latter.*

Our blindness is very often great at work, and God alone is aware of it. We permit ourselves to be conquered by illusions of sensibility, of character, of pride, of human respect. We substitute in place of good, of courage, of decorum, and of prudence whatever gives us satisfaction and seems naturally opportune. We can arrive at the point where we believe charity to be a sense of entirely human reckless extravagance, or an inclination of sympathy or passion. We imagine ourselves to be just when we are simply vindictive; to be courageous when we are simply indignant; and temperate when we are simply greedy and stingy.

We fool ourselves that what is evil is not really evil, merely because we are doing it; and out of pride, the evil we have committed seems to us a measure of fairness and sagacity. We assume that no one would think differently than we do, and we look with contempt on those who disagree with our assessments. We are convinced that the miseries of worldliness are requisites of civilization, and we consider ourselves models of balance between extremes, when in reality we are simply full of ourselves, and intolerant of anyone who contradicts us. We use every excuse available to justify our own conduct, and disguise our vices or lack of virtue, ascribing to them rationale and poise.

In arriving at these conclusions, we accept as light, the interior suggestions of Satan; and we stubbornly cling to a way which is not of God and does not lead to God, even wrapping ourselves in the mantle of sanctity. Under this aspect, we may say that the lack of Counsel is the most dangerous plague of our interior and exterior life, and exposes us to a thousand perils of sin, and to perdition.

The gift of Counsel gives to the soul a supernatural light which makes it see clearly if the promptings of reason or of the heart come from nature or from grace. It makes it see, for example, that complaints about the sins and defects of one's neighbor are not zeal, but resentment; that to respond to injuries and torts with bitter words is not justice or personal defense, but anger, hatred and vendetta; that to denigrate the works of others is not discretion, but envy; that to be fussy about food is not an exigency of health, but gluttony; that excessive concern for economy is avarice; that the quest for one's own decorum is pride and vanity; that the satisfaction of certain sensibilities and natural curiosities, and the same false love for certain creatures, is lust and impurity; that what is believed to be sobriety and a sense of moderation in religious exercises is not balance, but boredom.

A soul who has received the gift of Counsel constantly walks in the living splendor of a supernatural light, sees to the very core of every prompting of the heart, and uncovers all the malice nesting there, and all the tricks of Satan or illusions of a corrupt nature. The soul experiences a strong, interior impulse whereby it finds the power to face the truth and repress the promptings of nature, and can attain a wonderful purity of heart and a true holiness of life.

The soul experiences the inspiration and promptings of the Holy Spirit as an interior voice which speaks to it and makes it hear the voice of justice and righteousness. This is the voice so often grossly mistaken for one's own thought or for the voice of one's own conscience. People say: *My thought tells me: do not do this because it is bad,* when in reality it is the voice of the Holy Spirit which has suggested this. This voice, this internal inspiration which dissipates our illusions and rectifies our thoughts, is tender and persuasive, such that the soul feels charmed to follow it, and halts on the very edge of an abyss, like the son who hears the voice of his father, distinguishes it clearly among a thousand others, and follows it affectionately.

The soul which listens to this interior voice ceases to trust itself, and yields to the continuous direction of the Holy Spirit. This abandonment is one of the greatest of graces and the ultimate term to which the gift of Counsel leads the soul. The Holy Spirit then governs and directs the affections of the heart, takes possession of it, and establishes there a perfect and imperturbable tranquility, provided the soul follows his light and his promptings, and represses the promptings of nature at their onset. The Lord reigns as sovereign in this heart and fills it with his holy affections, whose ardor sometimes lasts for entire days and nights without any interruption.

The Holy Spirit governs and directs the soul's activities and external exercises. He works in the soul which abandons itself to him, as he did with the people of Israel when they went out of Egypt: so as not to lose their way, *The Lord went before the people to show the way by day in a pillar of cloud, and by night in a pillar of fire* [Ex 13: 21]. The Holy Spirit shows the soul, by an interior light, what it must practice, what is more perfect, and what will be more pleasing to him. He governs and directs the virtues, in such wise that where he rules, nothing mediocre is tolerated. He rouses the soul to virtue and to more heroic activities with such strong interior lights that everything seems easy.

The soul, consequently, carries its crosses with joy; promptly obeys in the most despised of services and work; tranquilly endures disdain, insult and humiliation; blesses God in the most bitter of tribulation; does good to those who do it evil; and loves those who are adverse to it.

We may say that the gift of Counsel is the great secret of the interior holiness of souls and of their saving activity for the benefit of others. This gift, then, *is necessary* for all the more important and more difficult situations, where eternal salvation and one's own sanctification is at stake, for example: one's vocation, or certain occasions of sin encountered in the exercise of one's profession and office. This gift is necessary at critical moments of life when we cannot entrust ourselves to human reason, so uncertain, so subject to error, so slow in its intuitions and decisions. It is especially necessary for superiors and priests, both as regards their own sanctification and that of others.

It is extremely difficult to reconcile with the apostolate, one's interior life; to reconcile with perfect chastity, the affection one must have for souls; to reconcile the simplicity of the dove, with the prudence of the serpent; so much so that without a light and a prompt guidance of the Holy Spirit, one is simply powerless to walk *the right path*. This light, therefore, let us repeat it, is above all necessary for superiors, because they must maintain discipline and at the same time keep the confidence and affection of their subjects. They must conciliate a just severity with kindness, maintain order without multiplying regulations, notifications and recommendations which are extremely annoying and provoke reactions in subjects. And then in the internal forum, how much discretion *spiritual directors* have need of to guide souls steadily and kindly, to enlighten them on their choice of a state in life; to make the yoke of the Lord sweet for them, and free them from the deceptions of temptations and fantasy!

It is necessary to realize that the greater number of souls are foolish and, at times, their judgments and ways of thinking are immature so as to act imprudently and compromise their standing before God and men, bringing many evils upon others, especially when they have the responsibility of guiding them. Tragically, the gift of Counsel is completely, or almost completely, wanting in the rulers of the peoples, and for this reason, nations are ruined and overpowered by irresponsible and stupid extremist movements.

We must ponder our own incompetence and recognize, with humble sincerity, the errors into which we so easily fall; and therefore, cultivate this gift of Counsel with great exactitude, first of all by imploring it of the Holy Spirit with fervent and incessant prayer each day. It is very useful to appeal to the Holy Spirit, via ardent ejaculations, for help and light during the day; to supplicate Jesus in the Blessed Sacrament to send His Spirit to us; and the Virgin Most Holy to draw the Spirit upon us by Her prayers, as She did upon the Apostles gathered in the Cenacle.

To such ardent and continuous prayer, it is necessary to unite a profound recognition of our misery and of our foolishness. The Holy Spirit lowers himself to the humble and resists the presumptuous and proud [cf. I Pet 5: 5]. He who trusts in his own judgment and in his own wisdom, cannot receive the light of the Holy Spirit, because, even if receiving it, he would throw it away; or in the best of hypotheses, would entangle it in his own darkness so as to render it inefficacious. How numerous are the mistakes we have made in our lives – and continue to make – that we should not! How many times have we been in danger because of our ineptitude? Let us, then, invoke the Counsel of the Holy Spirit and be attentive to his inspirations, without allowing ourselves to be guided by human, material, and opportunistic considerations.

The best counselors, said Donoso Cortes in his *Essays on Catholicism*, are the contemplatives, because they more than all others are led by the gift of Counsel. They have imperturbable good sense, true sagacity, wonderful dispositions for giving practical solutions to difficult problems; and in every question, address the key point, even if not particularly endowed with learning and human culture.

St. Catherine of Siena, for example, though very young and without education, gave wise counsel to princes, cardinals, and even to popes. St. Joan of Arc, ignorant of military arts, devised plans of war admired by the best military leaders, and indicated whence she had attained such wisdom, telling her judges: *You have consulted your council, and I, too, have consulted mine.* St. Gerard Majella was a simple Redemptorist lay brother, yet he offered enlightened, spiritual direction to many nuns and, oftentimes, other religious and priests; and even some bishops sought his counsel.

O HOLY SPIRIT God, conquer my stupidity and by thy Counsel make me wise; with thy gift make me docile to thy Counsel, and make me correspond to thy gift by abandoning myself to thy divine guidance. I am a poor, blind soul and I do not know my own heart; I deceive myself and I am my own seducer. Enlighten me, strike my heart, pull me from the abyss of my torpor and guide me. O infinite Love, O eternal Will of God, allow me to be carried by thee, and accomplish in me and in my life, the designs of thy divine Will. This is the true wisdom of life, as this is the summit of eternal life: *to do the divine will.* With thy light, I know that will; with thy counsel, I follow it; with thy grace, I fulfill it: *Veni, Sancte Spiritus! Come, Holy Spirit!*

VIII. Gift of Fortitude: Its Activity and Object – Necessity – Cultivation

The gift of Fortitude is thus defined: *A gift of the Holy Spirit which perfects the virtue of courage, giving to the will an impulse and an energy which renders it capable of suffering joyfully and intrepidly, and of accomplishing great projects, overcoming all obstacles.*

It differs from the virtue of courage, because it does not originate with our powers assisted by grace, but from a powerful action of the Holy Spirit which attracts the soul on high, withdraws it from the dark atmosphere of the earth, and makes it master of the lower faculties and of external difficulties encountered during laborious tasks. It reduces to naught the pessimism so often dominating the soul; overcomes hesitation in making decisions, fear in the face of obstacles, anxiety because of past failure, inertia in taking initiative; confers on the soul resolution, security, joy, and certainty of success; it spurs the soul to act and makes it ready to suffer heroically.

For this reason, it was said that the proto-martyr, St. Stephen, *was full of grace and power,* precisely because when he worked signs and wonders, and when he was dragged before the Sanhedrin, he was *filled with the Holy Spirit* [Acts 6:8; 7:55]. He had the gift of Fortitude when at work and when he faced his judges, as well as in his supreme sacrifice. *To work and to suffer* in the midst of the most painful difficulties with heroic effort and courage: the two acts to which the gift of Fortitude leads us.

To work – namely, to undertake the most arduous tasks without hesitation or fear; to practice perfect recollection in a most active life, as did St. Vincent de Paul and St. Teresa of Jesus; to preserve inviolate one's chastity in the most compromising circumstances, as did St. Thomas Aquinas and St. Charles Borromeo; to remain humble in the midst of honors and poor in spirit in the midst of plenty, as did the holy kings; to brave boredom, fatigue, dangers, and death, as did St. Francis Xavier; to ignore human respect and stand courageous in the face of tyrants, as did St. John Chrysostom.

To suffer – or to endure calmly and joyfully as well, long and painful illnesses, as did St. Ludwyna; to tolerate moral tribulations peacefully, whether calumny or persecution arising from without, or undergoing trials of purification within, which the Lord bestows on souls to refine them; to find oneself, as did the martyrs, in the throes of torture and violent death for the sake of truth, of virtue, of charity, and of the apostolate.

Martyrdom is considered the act *par excellence* of the gift of Fortitude, because with this supreme immolation, one gives to God what is most precious to oneself: life. But to overcome the serious difficulties that hinder doing good – to conquer them in the midst of opposition, calumnies, disdain, persecution, and humiliations of every kind – is also a form of martyrdom as to shed the blood of one's heart drop by drop.

Even on the plane of natural life, there are heroes: the brave who confront danger with courage or endure punishment and opposition to accomplish some undertaking for the advancement or benefit of mankind. Such heroism, however, although always the fruit of divine grace – because there is no such thing as a good work which does not come from God – is either born of the character, formation, or physical nature itself which God has given to certain individuals to fulfill a specific mission on earth. The gift of Fortitude, on the other hand, is neither an impetus nor a force, nor courage, nor natural stoicism; but it is the power of the Holy Spirit and the impulse of his love manifesting itself almost always in a fragile and weak nature, possessing something other than a fearless, strong, and resilient character.

Human heroism at times can also be an impetus bordering on the pathological, or which is indulged without immediate awareness of danger. The hero concentrates on the end to be accomplished and does not take into consideration the difficulties along the way to reach it. The warrior, for example, looks to the heights to be conquered and takes no account of the bursts of gunfire hindering his advancement; he rushes on, grasps nothing else, is filled with one thought; advances, not thinking of death, but of conquest; and if he should think of death, he moves aggressively against the enemy, for love of life, precisely to overcome him, because he knows that if he does not burst in and kill, he himself will be vanquished and killed.

Supernatural heroism, fruit of the gift of Fortitude, instead is calm, kind, circumspect, solid, and total, without pathological imbalance, because it commences with an impulse of Infinite Love, and has for its ultimate goal Infinite Love. It does not recognize the sensational, is always placid and sweet, and never contests the laws of charity.

As object, the gift of Fortitude does not only have exceptional moments in the life of the evidently heroic soul, but also bears with human weakness in every moment of life. It brings decisiveness and steadfastness to good works and overcomes obstacles impeding one's way.

Decisiveness and steadfastness are also fruits of the *virtue* of courage, but their activity is conditioned by human frailty, and is slow and spasmodic. The gift of Fortitude, on the contrary, renders those actions firm and without hesitation. The *virtue* may be likened to a kind of traction effected by hand or with a nag; the *gift* resembles that effected with a motor, as with a powerful automobile. The whip is needed to make the nag move forward; it strains to pulls the weight, sweats, labors, and has need of encouraging voices to motivate it. An automobile or motor, on the other hand, attached to the heavy cargo, will suffice to move it, overtake long miles with rapid speed, and overcome obstacles along the journey.

The gift of Fortitude, moreover, *makes a man strong and constant in the execution of holy resolutions*, and hence enables him to overcome the most dangerous of dead points in his spiritual life. There is nothing easier, in fact, than to make holy resolutions. Even the most tepid souls make them, either during the course of a retreat, or when they feel the weight of some chastisement by God, or some imminent danger consequent on their sins or their miseries. How long, however, do such good resolutions last? Human weakness and inconstancy are great, and when it comes to putting into practice a good resolution, we note how this is beyond our strength. It is easy to propose to accept adversity from the hand of God, as a disposition of his holy Providence; it is easy to propose not to lose one's temper, not to react, not to murmur, to bear with an annoying person, to overcome gluttony, to conquer suggestions to impurity, to desire not to look at immodest things, etc.; but when it comes to practice, our resolutions show themselves to be simply wishful thinking. It is the gift of Fortitude which makes us easily conquer these weaknesses of our nature.

By his intimate prompting, he does away with our natural resistance, sets our inmost being entirely at rest, and enkindles the fire of his love so intensely in our soul, that it desires at any price nothing other than the love of God. Then the soul experiences the firm and continuous will to work, to do the greatest violence to conquer itself [cf. Mt 11: 12]. It undertakes the practice of the most difficult virtues, without resenting the accompanying pain, because love makes everything tolerable and gives the soul such courage that it feels ready to give its very life as well, for Jesus Christ.

At times, the soul may notice in itself, periods of unexpected struggle which startle it, because the soul had presumed to have already vanquished its passions. Evil inclinations again surface, nature rebels, and the practice of virtue appears most difficult. The Lord permits these periods to purify the soul of hidden complacence in itself, at the very moment when the soul believes perseverance in doing good to be its almost connatural property. It is in such moments, however, that the gift of Fortitude is at work in the soul, and at that sign, the soul feels so reinvigorated by the Holy Spirit as to rise in spite of its own misery. It has recourse to penance, pours itself out in prayer, remains faithful and even desires the struggle in order to give witness of its own love to the Lord.

The gift of Fortitude makes a man strong and courageous in overcoming temptations, above all, those coming from the devil, which are insidious and most violent. The soul feels itself in danger, as the Apostles felt on the Lake of Genesareth [cf. Mt 8: 23–27; 14: 22–33], when they believed they were about to perish and every available aid seemed utterly inadequate. But just when the danger is greatest, the soul experiences in itself great confidence and strength; sensing itself fortified by a hidden power, it resists, overcomes, and remains tranquil.

The gift of Fortitude makes us strong and courageous in adversities; it liberates us from excessive sadness in the misfortunes of life and from the uncontrolled desire of being free, which can provoke a paralysis of despair if it is not granted. The soul, strengthened by the Holy Spirit, is sustained by a great trust in God; and in that sign, sensing the nearness of the Lord, the soul ends in loving and desiring suffering, and profoundly rejoicing in it, even though still immersed in it. The soul does not rejoice in suffering as such, because suffering is always repugnant to nature, but rejoices in it because, in suffering, it experiences a most profound union with God and can cry out with St. Teresa of Jesus: *Either suffer or die.*

This gift of Fortitude in suffering is poured out, in powerful fashion, even on the souls in purgatory. With an intensity beyond human comprehension, these souls suffer in the purifying flames, yet they have great joy and consolation, because they suffer out of love, and in suffering they are refined in love.

There remains a great question – the learned Fr. Luigi Da Ponte remarks – *to determine whether in Purgatory the pains and sufferings surpass the joy and consolation, or whether the joy and consolation surpass the pains and sufferings.* What can be said for certain is that the gift of Fortitude leaves the souls being cleansed, in perfect peace amidst the pains, and makes their joy superabundant by reason of their hope of glory, as St. Paul abounded in joy during his tribulations [cf. II Cor 1: 3–7].

THE GIFT OF Fortitude is supremely necessary both to lead a perfect Christian life and to advance along the ways of perfection. In many cases, in fact, preservation of the state of grace requires heroism, and this presupposes a super-human strength. To conquer oneself, one cannot simply walk the way of doing good, but must go against the current. Along with the inclinations moving us toward good, are others most violent and active which draw us toward evil; and to combat these, great strength of will, of love, and of virtue are needed. This strength comes to us from the Holy Spirit.

What generous efforts, indeed what heroic stress is postulated by the law of chastity to be observed throughout life! For those called to that state until marriage, it is necessary to practice absolute continence, under pain of mortal sin. Many young people do not marry until they are twenty-eight or thirty years old and, sadly, temptations against the beautiful virtue commence in adolescence and sometimes in childhood. This is a most grave danger, to be resisted at any cost, praying, keeping one's distance from dangerous reading, pictures and friendships; deploring even the slightest weaknesses, and picking oneself up immediately after falls. This presupposes effort and stress beyond the ordinary to control, where the gift of Fortitude is most necessary.

By means of this gift, the attacks of concupiscence, including those during marriage, are repressed. By means of this gift, one's nature is habituated to mortification, and the soul is raised up to heavenly desires and delights which lead it to despise those of the senses. For souls which have the good fortune and happiness to consecrate themselves to God, as do priests and religious, the gift of Fortitude is indispensable for them to vanquish the battle of the senses and to live on earth like angels.

Not only in the area of purity, but also for the other virtues, a special strength of the Holy Spirit is a prerequisite. Thus, to observe *justice* in financial, commercial, and industrial affairs during times of war and in the period immediately following, when there are so many occasions for violating it; to practice *justice* during times when competition and the urge to profit provoke sharp price increases beyond permissible limits, and often put a businessman in the dilemma of either being unjust or content with a low return; to resist the current fashion of cheating and of dishonest trade and instead remain faithful to the precepts of justice, requires greater than ordinary strength.

In addition to being necessary for the exercise and practice of purity, the gift of Fortitude is essential for priests and religious in order to fulfill the other duties of their state, because virtuous lives, demanding immolation and sacrifice, are entirely contingent upon this gift.

Fortitude is also vital to those professions requiring greater sacrifice than those of ordinary life; for instance, that of a physician, or of a soldier, whose circumstances expose him to every kind of danger; and in certain types of exhausting work which, via the sacrifices of those performing such labors, contributes to the common good and social welfare. For this reason – when the worker is not truly Christian and does not possess an interior, spiritual life to compensate for, and lighten his painful condition; when his mind is poisoned by wicked, atheistic propaganda and his heart is filled with hatred incited by Communism and Socialism – he becomes unhappy, restless, and despairing that he has to work for slave wages, and that his pay is never enough to provide for his needs or vices. Thus, he lives in an earthly hell, without peace and without the sweet hope of eternal happiness.

IF THE GIFT of Fortitude is so necessary to mortal life, it is urgent to cultivate it with great care because that life is a warfare and a trial [cf. Job 7:1]. First of all, it is important to implore this gift from the Holy Spirit every day, humbly acknowledging our impotence. The immense weakness and cowardice of so many worldly and religious souls in the fulfillment of their duties – above all, in the practice of purity, kindness, and mortification – is owing to the continued lack of beseeching God for the strength to practice such virtues.

This continuous prayer is also an alarm clock which keeps the soul watchful and on guard against dangers. When one is chosen by God to perform some difficult and extraordinary mission, still greater supplication for Fortitude is required, because being selected by God is not in itself a sign of the soul's ability or aptitude for such a mission, but exactly the contrary. It is written that *the foolish things of this world has God chosen to put to shame the wise, and the weak things to put to shame the strong, and the base things of the world and the despised and the things that are not, to bring to naught the things that are; lest any flesh should pride itself before him* [I Cor 1: 27–29]. Were the soul to glory or pride itself before him, it would remain within the limits of its own powers, and would never complete a greater and more ambitious task; the soul deeply needs to experience itself as impotent, weak, and impoverished to remain in God's hands as his instrument.

What is more inactive and totally inert than a brush in the hands of a painter? And could an artist ever paint with a brush capable of moving and squirming on its own? Could he, for example, use as a brush, the tail of a live lizard, which would continue to move and contort and wriggle in his hands? The soul which glories in itself is, like a lizard's tail, an excessively mobile instrument to serve God's purposes in the order of holiness; but the weak, impoverished, weary soul which acknowledges its own frailty, entrusting itself entirely to the power of God, is like a brush or instrument in the clasp of the artist and under his complete control.

The more the instrument is impoverished yet docile, all the more does the artist totally love it as his own and holds it dearly as a treasure, even if it appears base in the eyes of someone who does not grasp the exigencies of his design and of artistic creativity. But should the chosen instrument still possess something of its own, for example, a tuft of hair sticking out from the brush, or knots in the handle making it difficult to manipulate – so, even before using it, the artist makes it undergo a kind of suffering: he cuts off the tuft and files down the knots. Next, he carefully sands the handle and trims off needless length so as to control the excessive swelling of hairs, and to bring it under his complete control in the performance of his art. If the brush had intelligence, would it continuously complain against the artist who properly maintains it and skillfully accomplishes that which, of its own, it cannot do? Left to its own devices, it would fall and, on impact, would simply create an indistinct blob on the canvas.

Thus, are we in the hands of God. Should he, out of his goodness, gives us our freedom, and if our freedom can only support us at the low level of our nature, we have need of his power to raise ourselves to his height; we have need of trials and tribulations to refine us; of profound humility to remain docile in his hands and accomplish that which he wants us to realize, making use of us so as to glorify us as objects of his love.

God manifests his omnipotence in working through us since, in his hands, there is no instrument as mobile as a free man. Intelligence, will, freedom, body, senses, nerves, our miserable company, our sins, meanderings, foolishness – our entire being is a dizzying mobility. Because God makes use of it, we must be lovingly controlled by his power; by his habitual grace which puts us in order; by actual grace which moves us; by the gift of Fortitude which strengthens and activates us in him.

The gift of Fortitude, therefore, is one of the capstones of our supernatural life, and must be implored continuously of God. In Confession and at Communion especially, we can attain that power which we need to overcome our nature and triumph over all the obstacles which act as blocks to our supernatural life. From Confession, we emerge renewed and purified, our freedom properly ordered and our will strengthened, and from the Sacred Table, as St. John Chrysostom says, *we return as lions, breathing flames of love, terrifying to Satan.*

To CULTIVATE THE gift of Fortitude, it is necessary to daily take advantage of all the small occasions for vanquishing self by practicing patience. A soldier, a boxer, an athlete, acquires the habit of courage via gymnastics; we acquire it via patience, discipline of life and penance which are part of patience. Those who act thusly make themselves subject to a rule requiring them to be devout in prayer, recollected during the day, and silent when they would prefer to chat. They avoid looking at objects that arouse curiosity, put up with inclement weather and cold or hot seasons without complaint; they display courtesy to those who are naturally unpleasant and, do so without feigning for the sake of social appearances, but rather for love of God and out of charity.

They train and conquer themselves to attain Fortitude, drawing to themselves this gift of the Holy Spirit. They patiently and humbly accept reproofs, and adapt themselves to the tastes of others, as well as to their desires and whims; they bear contradictions calmly and, in a word, strive to vanquish themselves and triumph over their passions. If they do all this, not merely once in passing, but habitually; and if they do it, not only patiently, but joyfully for love of God, they are already heroic; and it will not be difficult for them to be exceedingly heroic in the gravest of circumstances that might arise, because such persons already possess the Fortitude of the Holy Spirit.

COME, O HOLY Spirit of God! Support our weakness; with thy Fortitude, make us victorious in our struggles! Thou art the Spirit of peace and of calm in the midst of tempests – do thou enable us to control them; thou art the Spirit of consolation and of joy in the midst of disappointments – do thou enable us to vanquish them; thou art the Spirit of magnanimity and strength amidst crosses – do thou make us embrace them. Come thou, and sustain our weakness; make us fearless against opposition, heroic amidst trials, generous in pardoning and in patience, always with heart turned toward eternal glory and eternal peace: *Veni, Sancte Spiritus!*

IX. *Gift of Knowledge: True Knowledge and the Science of the Saints – Object and Necessity of the Gift of Knowledge – Cultivation*

The knowledge of which we speak is not *philosophic* science acquired by reasoning, nor *physical* science in its multiple branches, experimental and positive, acquired by the study of creation and of the laws which govern it, and neither is it *theological* knowledge acquired through study of revelation and through intense reasoning about the data of faith. It is rather the *Science of the saints*. This is the true and supreme *speculative* science, because it enables us to reach the supreme causes in all branches of knowledge, and makes us correctly assess all created things in relation to God. It is the true and supreme *positive* science, because it rests on the *perfectly positive* supreme truth and on his Providence, and because it is *experienced* with the most positive method of research which is to *live* what we know.

Nothing is in fact more positive *than the life we live*, both materially and spiritually; nothing is more *experiential* than, for example, the beating of one's own heart and the profound affections of one's own soul and conscience. Nothing is more true than *the eternal truth*, known by Faith, confirmed by the wonderful Magisterium of the Church – *lived* in the intimate life of the soul; *assessed* by the life of the souls who have lived or live; *confirmed* by experience and by the history of the ages; splendidly *illumined* by the evidence of miracles and of supernatural revelations – which makes it the *science of the most positive of phenomena* and the irrefutable and unmistakable *intuition* of truth.

We propose to speak here of this wonderful Science – absolutely true, fully real and positive, complete without shadow of error, distortion, illusion, false experience, mistaken intuition – all of which otherwise falls into historical obsolescence like withered leaves in autumn. This Science can and must be the patrimony of every soul, because all are made for eternal life. This Science constitutes true joy in living, outside of which or without which, everything becomes dark and saddening, as a journey in the dead of night saddens and becomes a mass of frightful shadows. Of this Science all the other sciences are handmaids, which either find in it the compass enabling them to bear positively on the truth, or without which, they become toys or play things to entertain, kill time, and bring one to the finish line of death without even minimal hope.

What is a scientific toy? – It is a mechanism that presupposes a superior mechanic; its purpose, however, is limited to a few idle moments of brief amusement for a boy; when it becomes worn out from use or damaged by the child, it no longer functions and, being of no further service, is tossed in the trash. So too, is prideful and renowned human science without faith, or worse, against the Faith; materialistic science, or what is sometimes called scientism, is relegated to this state, yet remains the object of adoration by atheists and non-believers!

The gift of Science of which we speak, therefore, holds the greatest spiritual and material interest for both the individual and for society as a whole. In the sequence of the gifts of the Holy Spirit chronicled by the Prophet Isaiah – and acknowledged by the Church – the gift of Science stands precisely between the gifts of Fortitude and of Godliness as light of our earthly life; for it is that light which strengthens us in the Faith while living on earth; and in our relations with God, it activates us in works of faith and love.

The gift of Knowledge is thus defined: *A gift which under the illuminating action of the Holy Spirit, perfects the virtue of faith, making us know created things in relation to God, and making us see promptly and surely what regards our sanctification and that of others.*

Before every other consideration, let us ponder well, the profound words of the Ven. Olier, who makes us better understand and justifies what we have just said about science. Let us ponder indeed, because the true root of modern apostasy from God, resulting in the decay of Christian nations, is ascertained here in deceptive knowledge, be it agnostic or atheistic. This knowledge has poisoned the modern mind-set and has led hearts astray.

The learned and devout Olier writes: "*God is a being who fills and occupies all. He appears under the facade of all things. In the heavens and on earth he tells us something about what He is… Whence in every creature, which is as it were a sacrament of the perfections of God, we must adore him whom it represents… We would easily succeed in doing just this, were it not for having lost the grace of Adam…. But sin robbed us of this knowledge, nor has it been restored except in Jesus Christ, who confers it on very pure souls, for whom faith unveils the majesty of God wherever found…. This light of faith is properly called the science of the saints, and without the help of the senses, without the experience of reason, manifests the dependence on God found in every creature… This is a knowledge acquired without fatigue and in an instant. With a sole glance it penetrates to the cause of all things, and finds in every argument subjects for meditation, for perfect contemplation."*

Created things insofar as they lead to God are the *object* of the gift of Knowledge. If we consider their origin, they tell us that their source is in God who created and conserves them; if we study their nature, we discover an image or reflection of God; finally, their end is that of leading us to God, and they as so many steps which ascend to him. In looking at created things simply, and still more in pondering their harmony and in studying their laws, the soul remains absorbed in love for God, contemplates his wisdom, admires his goodness, exalts his glory, and senses a need to further deepen its knowledge of creatures so as to praise their Creator more profoundly.

With this sublime Science, creation no longer appears a mute scene, but is wholly and entirely a wonderful canticle, conferring on the soul a true and profound joy and happiness. Thus did St. Francis of Assisi consider creatures, and seeing them also as daughters of the supreme Father, he called them sisters [cf. his *Canticle of the Creatures*]. The unshakeable solidity of the mountains made him immediately recognize the strength of God and what support it offers us; the appearance of a flower, in its freshness and in its odor, revealed to him the purity and infinite beauty of God, on account of which he was deeply moved and at times shed tender tears.

If men had not been miserably degraded by sins, and especially by the sin of impurity, they would have in creation an inexhaustible font of sublime sights, a wonderful scenario of genuine entertainment of the spirit. From these sights, by means of the gift of Knowledge, they would have felt drawn to still more immensely beautiful sights, to God himself, font of peace and of love. Instead, men have degraded themselves in their senses. They have thrown themselves like voracious hyenas on the carcasses of life, and lacking any enlightenment, they focus their wretched attention on shameful nudity, not even to admire the material beauty of the body, but merely to further abase themselves in the degradation of sin and perish in the bogs of vice, suffocating from the pace of a deceptive life, as an unfortunate happens upon quicksand is overwhelmed and swallowed up.

We are blinded in life; we esteem and hold as great goods, things which are poison for us, and despise as great evils, things which are the better means of salvation. Confused by this blindness, we love what we ought to hate, and hate what we should love. We are in extreme need of being deprogrammed and guided, if we want to save ourselves. The Holy Spirit, with his gift of Knowledge, communicates to the soul a supernatural light which makes it perceive not only the vanity, but also the danger of all things which the world esteems and loves. The soul then becomes like a blind man who has recovered his sight; it sees created things, not in some illusory or imaginative way, but for what they are before God; the soul no longer crashes – like the blind stumbling over a barrier intended to guide or protect, or on a sidewalk designed to provide safe boundaries – but rather, sees in an instant the purpose of the barrier and sidewalk, and marches more expeditiously toward the goal.

The material world in which we live, and everything that it contains, for all its beauty and natural wonder, is not the goal of our life. With the gift of Knowledge, the Holy Spirit makes us experience, via admiration of created things, the desire for eternal beauty, guides our will, inflames our love; and then the soul does not stop at created things, but admires in them the Creator and desires him above all else.

The gift of Knowledge does not only make us see created things in their relation to God, but makes us promptly and surely see that which regards our salvation and that of others. This gift enlightens us on the state of our soul, on its secret movements, its principles, its motives, and on the consequences which might be derived thereof. It also teaches us how to deal with our neighbor in regard to his eternal salvation; thus, a preacher is enlightened by this gift to deliver a message that will benefit the assembly; a director is enlightened on how to guide souls, according to their spiritual needs and the movements of grace, by penetrating into the depths of their hearts. This particular aspect of the gift of Knowledge constitutes what is known as *discernment of spirits* by which many saints came to know the most secret thoughts of their penitents, even before they had been revealed.

FROM WHAT HAS been said, we see clearly that the gift of Knowledge has two operations in the soul: – *1)* It makes the soul know created things in their relation to God and elevates the soul from creation to the Creator. – *2)* It makes the soul know what regards its sanctification and that of others, and orientates the soul in the assessment of its judgments and in the movements of its will.

We may say that – as in human science one distinguishes between physical science which explores creation, and philosophical and moral science which should orient our thought and moral conscience – so it is, with the gift of Knowledge that the Holy Spirit gives us light for knowing the relation of created things to God; therefore, giving us increased knowledge in regard to their purpose; and light for orienting our thoughts, conscience, and will in the way of perfection. This is a totally admirable, divine and moral philosophy which brings the soul to sanctity and salvation.

By means of the gift of Knowledge, then, the soul does not only become ecstatic over creation, elevating itself to God, but also avoids the risk of becoming deeply absorbed in created things. The soul senses itself detached from creatures, knowing by the light of the Holy Spirit, how vain they are in themselves and utterly deficient for making one happy. It sees the great danger creatures present, and recognizes the potential for being perversely attracted to them, resulting in its seduction and separation from God. Knowing creation in God and for his glory, and valuing created things as nothing in contrast with those eternal, the soul orientates itself to this life; judges surrounding elements rightly and prudently; despises what should be despised; and embraces those supernatural means which guide it to salvation. This is what we have called *the Science of the saints*, the only true science which makes man wise and elevates him.

It is necessary to cultivate this gift and beseech it of the Holy Spirit, renewing our faith and elevating our soul to God in our daily actions and in our manner of looking upon creatures. All creation is the praise of God and our soul must be like a harmonium where this praise resounds, like a flowering hillside where the echo is heard, in such wise that *no wonder among the works of God leaves us indifferent, and none as ignorant admirers those who gape at an anonymous work.*

If we admire a work of art by Michelangelo, we praise him; why then, when looking upon the works of the Lord do we not praise him who is their most wise and loving maker? We must recognize what an abominable affront is the modern-day practice of not ascribing to God even the remotest link in matters of science! Never a reference to him in the study of the heavens; never an avowal of his wisdom in anatomical studies of the human body; not a single act of grateful love for the innumerable creatures he has placed at our service! Why this shocking omission? The reason is that so many are fearful of being thought bigots – as if the glorification of God is not the most supreme and honorable occupation in life!

Let us habituate ourselves to consider the vanity of material things we so easily become attached to; let us learn how to deprive ourselves of a curious glance, an idle reading, a bit of food, or of some diversion or satisfaction – in other words, how to sacrifice to God. These small victories over self, prepare and open our soul to the gift of the Holy Spirit, making us docile to his sanctifying action and capable of efficaciously influencing others to holiness.

COME, O HOLY Spirit, enlighten me that I might live in the light of faith, and not be conquered by the spirit of the world, which is the spirit of apostasy and of indifference. Come, and place on my lips the canticle of all the creatures, as you placed it on the lips of St. Francis of Assisi: – Praise the Lord from the heavens, praise him in the heights. Praise him all ye, his hosts. Praise him, O sun, O moon; praise him, O stars, all ye shining lights… Praise him, all ye his wondrous works; praise him for the immensity of his majesty [Ps 148]. – Come, guide me in the ways of love; detach me from all that is earthly; make me love the Cross, and crying out like a banished exile aspire to that great flight which must terminate at the very throne of God! Come, send forth into me a ray of thy heavenly light to illumine me, that I might live in God and for God and glorify him in time and in eternity: – *Veni, Sancte Spiritus!*

X. Gift of Godliness: Its Nature – Effects – Necessity For All and Especially for Priests and Religious – Cultivation

The gift of Godliness [also called Piety] perfects the virtue of religion which is annexed to justice. Religion *is a moral, supernatural virtue, which inclines the will to render to God the worship due him for his infinite excellence and for his supreme dominion over us.* It is an act of highest justice to give to God the adoration, love and honor which is owed him as Creator and as our Father. The gift of Godliness is thus defined: *a gift which produces in the heart a filial affection for God and a tender devotion to persons and to things divine, to make us perform our religious duties with holy care.*

The virtue of religion is acquired through determined effort, and to facilitate its acquisition, the gift of Godliness is given to us by the Holy Spirit. The virtue of religion is a kind of profound deference a subject renders to a king by diligently observing court etiquette which, little by little, develops into that respect known as loving care and fidelity. The gift of Godliness resembles the profound tenderness a son feels for his father, a quasi-spontaneous act of the heart which induces expressions of loving respect for him and for those dear to him, whom he loves. Hence, the gift of Godliness makes us see in God not only the supreme Lord, but the best and most loving of fathers, and expands our hearts with confidence and love. It, therefore, produces in us:

1) – A filial respect for God, which makes us adore him with tender and holy care, as a most beloved Father, and leads us to consider exercises of piety not as burdensome occupations, but as a need of the soul and as a leap of the heart toward God.

2) – A generous love for God, which to please him brings us to sacrifice ourselves for him and for his glory. It is not, then, an egoistic piety seeking consolations; an indolent piety remaining idle when it should be working; an exclusively sentimental piety in search of an emotional charge, abandoning itself to fantasy; it is a virile piety which manifests love by doing the will of God.

3) – An affectionate obedience which sees in the precepts and evangelical counsels, the expression of God's will for us, and prods the soul to observe them; it produces full abandonment into the hands of this loving Father, who always works out of love, and proves us to purify us of our weaknesses and unite us to him.

The soul does not become perturbed by the obscurities and mysteries of Providence, nor even by those regarding phenomena of the universe and animal life. The soul does not assess these enigmas by human or personal criteria, and is neither bewildered by them, but recognizes *that God is good and does all well,* and leaves to him alone, the government of his creatures. The soul knows that God is charity, love, and goodness; and so to think that ice can be found in fire, is as absurd to think that in him and in his Providence, there can be anything wrong, or worse, cruel. The soul is sure of God, trusts in him, and loves him with great tenderness, even in the midst of sorrow and suffering. It is precisely in trials and obscurity that the soul gives to the Lord, the most tender witness of fidelity and love.

It is necessary to deepen still further these characteristics of the gift of Godliness and to implore it of the Holy Spirit with greater ardor, since quite often, by reason of either diabolic temptation or superficiality in thought, certain souls harbor in their inmost selves a diffidence, if not veiled hostility toward the Lord, which produces in them insensitivity and hardness of heart. In theory they believe that God is infinitely good, and that he is worthy of an infinite love for his own sake; they believe that God is this infinite love who has given us all that we have and all that we are, out of pure mercy; they believe that God is our last end, and that every joy, every pleasure, every good in this life and in the next consists in possessing him and loving him. But for all that, they remain hard, insensitive, wanting in piety and true devotion, wanting in love and tenderness for God, because they do not have the gift of Godliness and neglect to call it down upon themselves.

The holy king and prophet David, who had received this gift in its fullness, and who in his Psalms, had poured out his heart to the Lord in so many ways, said that *his heart has become as wax, it melts in my bowels* [Ps. 21: 15]. In reality the gift of Godliness works in the heart as fire on wax: fire softens wax and renders it malleable, capable of taking any desired form. Fire melts wax and poured into a mold, the wax turns into a lovely form.

With his gift, the Holy Spirit softens the soul and impresses on it, together with a sense of great tenderness, the concept of God's grandeur and of his love; he impresses on the soul, together with a sense of compassion or of profound joy, Jesus despised or Jesus glorified; Jesus abandoned on the

Cross or waited on by Angels in the desert; Jesus disfigured in the Passion or Jesus supremely captivating in His infancy. The gift of Godliness softens the insensitivity of the soul, and gives it a devotion so tender, and a longing so ardent for God and for all that can tend to his honor and love, that the soul feels immersed in an ocean of happiness. The soul's darkness comes to be filled with a loftier light, brightening everything; restlessness departs and the heart is left in quiet serenity; in place of dryness and insensitivity, the gentleness of divine love enters in and radiates throughout the heart.

This gentleness and this internal peace also make the soul gentle and amiable toward its neighbor, because the love of God is inseparable from love of neighbor. If the heart, in fact, were to experience affection and tenderness only toward God, without consideration as well for neighbor, the image of God, its piety would be deceitful, or at best only a sensible devotion which would quickly vanish. This inseparable double love makes the soul generous toward God and compassionate toward neighbor. The soul is ready for any sacrifice so as not to displease the Lord, so as to make reparation for the offenses which He receives from men. The soul thus becomes generous toward neighbor, with an all maternal tenderness, taking that neighbor's sufferings within itself as though its own, so as to even forget its own interests. The soul in possession of the gift of Godliness is without contempt, without discontent, and without outbursts of passion; such a soul does not complain, does not murmur, does not nurture antipathy for its neighbor, always seeks peace, and is supremely affable.

The gift of Godliness gives us tender love and kindness for neighbor, because it makes us love persons and things which partake of the being and perfections of God; its action and influence on the soul have therefore a greater scope, and are not merely restricted to our neighbor. In virtue of this gift, we venerate and love the Most Holy Virgin as Mother of God and our Mother, and with moving devotion, offer to Her something of that veneration and love that we have for God, inasmuch as among creatures, She is that one who best reflects the divine perfections. We exult in Her as children; we have recourse to Her as Mother full of grace; we take refuge in Her as our Advocate; and we invoke Her as treasurer of all graces.

In virtue of the gift of Godliness, we love and venerate the Angels for the wondrous charm of their nature and beauty; we love the saints, appreciating their virtues and seeking to imitate them. We love the Church as bride of Jesus Christ and our Mother, and we live of Her life as of the life of Jesus Christ. We live in full and perfect obedience to those who govern the Church, especially to the Pope, in whom we see and, we may add, venerate the Vicar of Jesus Christ. In virtue of the gift of Godliness Holy Writ is for us the word of God, on which we meditate, not in the letter, in a human way, but in the spirit, applying it to our life.

From what we have said, it is evident that Christians are greatly in need of the gift of Godliness to fulfill their duties of Religion toward God, of respectful obedience toward superiors, and of joyful and thoughtful consideration for inferiors. Without this gift, they would deal with God, as with a patron, in a servile spirit and not out of love; their faith would be a desert. Prayer, without the blooms of delicacy and love, would bring them burden, rather than consolation, as one can sadly verify in so many souls. To those lacking this gift, providential trials would seem a harsh, even unjust, chastisement. Without it, Christians would live in a dark and pessimistic atmosphere, plodding along the way of the spirit – except for fleeting moments of fanciful exhilaration – giving a little to the world, a little to God, a little to nature, and a little to the spirit.

This gift is indispensable for priests, religious, and all persons in the world, consecrated to God. In fact, without it, the numerous retreats which form the warp and woof of their life, would become an intolerable yoke, because it is not possible to reflect on God at length, unless one loves him. Who can study a science in depth, without experiencing some kind of overwhelming emotion? And what artist could cultivate his talent, without a burst of love and passion? What passion is, in a natural activity, the gift of Godliness is, in spiritual and supernatural activities.

This gift is also indispensable in treating others with charity and delicacy, especially when individuals are unfriendly, demanding, or hostile. The exercise of good manners is not adequate strategy to succeed in negative encounters; and still less, is the use of diplomacy, or of a disingenuous approach which, tactically, is a greater affront than a direct insult. The gentleness of charity, the profound respect for neighbor out of love for God, and taking pity on the weaknesses of others are required; and these are the fruits of the gift of Godliness. By means of this gift, superiors become fathers; equals become brothers; the little ones and subjects become our children; the suffering and the poor become the privileged part of our heart and the object of our tenderness.

It is, therefore, necessary to cultivate this gift of the Holy Spirit, often meditating on the events and texts of Scripture which bespeak the mercy and kindness of God; and to read either the lives of the saints who depict these virtues, or classical and devotional literature which make us deepen our understanding of them. It is extraordinarily beneficial for the soul to see, for example, how God has responded with miracles, and how he continues to reward that confidence which the saints place in him. It is extremely moving and spiritually instructive for the soul to ponder the mercy God bestows upon the sinful soul when it returns to him with a repentant heart.

In addition it is necessary to be faithful and constant in the exercises of piety, both in those commanded by the Church, and in our particular devotions. Infidelity or inconstancy produces idleness in the soul and spiritual boredom, i.e., the two interior conditions which impede the action of the Holy Spirit in the soul, and which almost always produce hardening of the heart. One who seriously neglects obligatory prayer, destroys the spirit of piety in himself; and one who negligently overlooks a seriously obligatory act of supererogation, falls asleep and becomes spiritually idle, as an arm or hand kept abnormally immobile in one position, falls asleep.

To cultivate the gift of Godliness, it is also necessary to transform the ordinary actions of life into acts of religion, doing them to please the heavenly Father; in such wise, one's entire life becomes a prayer and, therefore, an act of filial piety toward God and of fraternal charity toward one's neighbor. St. Paul writes: *Train thyself in godliness. For bodily training is of little profit, while godliness is profitable in all respects, since it has the promise of the present life as well as of that which is to come* [I Tim 4: 7–8]. Training in the love of God and in conversation with him in prayer, habituates us to acts of profound devotion, and these make us exercise acts of love toward Our Lady and the saints, and acts of delicate affection for our neighbor.

COME, THEN, IN me, O Holy Spirit of God, and fill me with the gift of Godliness; give me a tender and filial love for God, that I might find in him alone all my pleasure, and adore all his arrangements. Come, and give me a great kindness and a sincere charity toward my neighbor, that I might admire in all men the image of God and recognize them as his sons and my brethren. Come, and give me a great love for my most sweet Mother Mary, for the angels and saints; make my soul take nourishment in the Church, as a daughter takes nourishment at her mother's breast. Come and fill me with thy love, O Holy Spirit God, that through thee I might live as a pilgrim on earth, and that in dying through thee, I might gain eternal beatitude. – *Veni, Sancte Spiritus!*

XI. Gift of the Fear of the Lord: Its Nature – Grandeur Within the Harmony of the Seven Gifts – Necessity – Cultivation

In speaking of the *Fear of the Lord*, we do not intend here, to treat of that "slavishly servile" fear, such as many experience when faced with temporal chastisements, nor of those they may also receive from the Lord; nor of that fear which people feel when assailed by some degree of misfortune or disaster, resulting from powerful – or worse – potentially harmful forces of unknown and mysterious nature. It is not our intention either, to deal with that dreadful fear of God which, at the mere remembrance of our sins, disturbs and depresses us in seeing him as the inexorable judge who cannot do other than condemn us. Neither are we dealing here with a fear of hell sufficient to initiate conversion, but one that would prevent conversion from culminating in sanctification. In our times, so lacking in faith, when people are accustomed to thinking of the terrible reality of hell as chimera, it is more plausible for them to confront fear of temporal chastisement rather than that of damnation, for the very reason that temporal chastisements have been witnessed and verified as documented events, sparing neither an epoch, nor country, nor year.

There is not a country or region which does not witness, for example, the catastrophes that strike those who profane the Cross, sacred icons, or the Eucharist. The misfortunes that befall those who purchase or appropriate ecclesiastical goods reserved for religious or in suffrage for the poor, are legendary. Even the worst of atheists and bigots fear obtaining goods or objects of the Church because they are afraid of being abased to beggary as a result of their deed. This fear rests on a fear of the Lord and recognition of his justice, but it is laced with superstition more than a genuine sentiment of faith. Because it does not extend beyond the limits of personal, material interests, it does not provide the least merit in detaching the soul from its sins, nor in attaining a steadfast conversion to God.

The Fear we want to focus on is *the reverential and filial fear* which leaves us frightened by every offense to God *because sin separates us from him.* Consequently, the soul's fright at staining itself by sin and of being overwhelmed with painful anxiety of conscience, cannot be called fear of the Lord, because such fear is more a preoccupation with one's own personal excellence, than a fear of lacking in reverence for God and of being separated from him through sin. Scrupulous souls, for example, are preoccupied with sin, which results in the ultimate fixation – morbidity – because by way of a hidden pride of the spirit, they flee from admitting any guilt in themselves. They cannot bear the thought of being recognized and labeled as sinners; they are terrified of having to accuse themselves of sin to a confessor. They are similar to those individuals who do not want to make a bad impression on society, and fuss to extreme over their appearance because they seek admiration and praise. The fear of scrupulous souls, therefore, is quite other than the fear of offending God and being separated from him. They are only concerned with themselves and preoccupied with their own perfection, if in fact, they are not mentally disturbed to some degree, as persons who are obsessed with cleanliness and fearful of infections or germs.

The Fear of the Lord, gift of the Holy Spirit, is defined thus: *A gift which inclines the will to filial respect for God, keeps us from sin because it displeases God, profoundly humiliates us before him, and makes us hope in his powerful assistance.* This gift perfects, at one and the same time, the virtues of *hope* and of *temperance.* It perfects the virtue of hope, making us take fright at displeasing God and being separated from him. Fear, in this case, makes us desire more intensely to be united with God in Paradise, since a person who fears to offend his beloved, naturally feels a desire to be near him in intimate friendship; and should one be far away from the beloved, living elsewhere for a time, he clings to the hope of seeing and dwelling with his beloved. The fear of the Lord perfects and promotes the virtue of temperance, because not wanting to displease God and longing to be united to him, we detach ourselves from false loves of the world and flee those amusements and those material satisfactions which could make us lose God.

The Fear of the Lord embraces three principal acts: – *1)* A living sense of the grandeur of God, and therefore a supreme horror of even the smallest sins which offend his infinite majesty. The saints, who were filled with this gift, deplored even their slightest faults and were not convinced they had ever done enough to make reparation for them. – *2)* The gift of Fear arouses the soul to a living sorrow for the very least faults committed because they offend an infinitely good God, and imparts to it a living desire to make reparation. – *3)* It gives the soul a vigilant concern to flee the occasions of sin, and a great diligence to know and perform the divine Will totally.

The perception which the soul has of the horror of sin and of every least fault, depends on the vivid light with which the Holy Spirit illumines it. As a lantern, on a dark night of a violent storm, pierces the clouds and brightens the horizon for a moment, so the light of the Holy Spirit, like a bright lantern, illumines the darkness of human incomprehension, and in the twinkle of an eye makes the soul see the filth of sin and conceive a great horror for it. In these moments of grace, the soul does not see anything else but sin, and were the soul to possess the whole world, it would be willing to lose that entire world to preserve the grace of God.

The horror of guilt which the soul experiences is not a passing sentiment, but is constant and deep in the soul itself, such that nothing can turn it from its resolutions. The soul keeps itself pure and lives in unswerving fidelity. Such a person falling into some venial sin, falls out of weakness and never out of willful and deliberate negligence. Such a person, once aware of his fall, makes reparation for it amid sighs and penitential groans.

The gift of the Fear of the Lord radically springs forth from Infinite Love and confers on the soul a flowering of true love of God. It is not the love which tastes the divine grandeurs, as in the gift of Wisdom. It is not the love which beatifies the truths of Faith in contemplation, as in the gift of Understanding. It is not the love which advances prudently along the difficult paths of the supernatural life and along those of the earthly pilgrimage, as in the gift of Counsel. It is not the strong love which combats and sacrifices, as in the gift of Fortitude. It is not the love which sees the glow of creation and its harmony in relation to heavenly things and to God himself, as in the gift of Knowledge. It is not the love displayed in tender intimacies which speaks, converses, and even plays with the Lord, as in the gift of Godliness; but it is an adoring love which conceives a most profound respect for the majesty of God, and feels overwhelmed by his greatness.

This love sees and appreciates the infinite superiority of God over all creatures, profoundly intent that he alone is worthy of every honor, and consequently experiences a most vivid repugnance for sin which robs that honor and defies the divine Will. By means of this love the soul seeks refuge from guilt, detests sin, makes reparation for it, expiates it, deplores it, and combats it with ardor and zeal, that no one would sin.

The gift of Fear of the Lord, therefore, far from being *the least perfect*, as some would classify it, in contrast with *the most perfect* which is the gift of Wisdom, is a gift which in Sacred Scripture is logically listed last, because by means of the concept it forms of God's grandeur and of his majesty, *it is a supernatural habit which gives to our life and to the faculties of the soul, such docility to God, as to obey promptly his laws*, which means flee sin and do good, *and inflames the soul with tender and respectful love for God*. Considered in its full extension, it is not the first step on the paths of love, but is one of those supernatural habits which lifts the soul to God.

In the gift of Wisdom the soul, while contemplating God, opens its eyes in ecstasy before him; in the gift of Fear, the soul, while adoring God's majesty, casts its eyes down. The soul is no less loving in lowering its eyes than when it opens them; just as the soul is not less loving when, docile to the light, to the power and tenderness of God, it examines his grandeurs with Understanding, receives his guidance with Counsel, glorifies his goodness and truth with Fortitude, exalts his creative power with Knowledge; and when apprizing him as first principle and last end, the soul throws itself on him with Godliness, and so lives in the calm and serene atmosphere of a living faith, glorifying God in divine worship and with canticles of love. With Wisdom the soul sees, with Understanding it scrutinizes, with Counsel it is directed, with Fortitude it labors for the glory of God, with Knowledge it recognizes him in all that is created; with Godliness, it speaks to God, and in adoring God, pours itself out on him. With Fear, the soul observes the proper distance which delineates the relationship between Creator and creature; it does not become self-confident which would incline it to treat with him as an equal; it feels his infinite majesty, senses the duty to adore him, and does not want to displease him at any price.

The Fear of the Lord is necessary, then, that the soul not take improper liberties with God and with holy things, that it not speak to the Lord with excessive boldness, and we might add, with less than good manners, unmindful of his infinite grandeur and the immeasurable chasm separating us from him. Even when God invites the soul to partake in the special gifts of a sweet and wondrous familiarity with himself, the soul must never forget to treat him with reverence and tender fear, and at the very least, with as much regard as would be displayed to a person of great dignity on earth who accords the soul his confidence. To have Jesus living and true in the Most Blessed Sacrament, to be able to treat with Him at the altar, take Him and guard Him on one's heart in carrying Him to the sick – as do priests, in virtue of the immense grace of their ministry – is not license to treat Him as though He were just anybody.

The Fear of the Lord also leads one to make a gesture of profound respect in handling the Sacred Species or the sacred vessels which contain them. There is the all-too-human and harsh manner of handling and guarding them which reveals a want of faith and of holy fear, as replacing the Pyx on the altar with a thud hard enough to break it, rather than gently setting it down; or placing the Sacred Theca on one's breast as though adjusting one's watch, without even the mere gentle touch it would take to warm a live chick on one's breast – manifesting both a lack of faith and love for Jesus Christ.

The soul which presents itself at the altar for Communion in a dissipated and distracted manner, barely genuflecting, receiving the Host as one would take any morsel of food – and still worse, approaching without modesty or composure – shows itself to have no Fear of the Lord and, therefore, has an even greater need for this gift of the Holy Spirit. Were one to receive a delicious confection, or an even more palatable delicacy, one would spontaneously respond with politeness and joyful courtesy in a manner suitable to accepting something of a special treat, rather than an ordinary piece of bread or fruit.

To receive Jesus without courtesy, modesty, and good manners, which so great a gift requires, is something unworthy, but unfortunately, very common among modern Christians. We priests, who are familiar with the distribution of the Most Blessed Sacrament by reason of the exercise of our ministry, sorrowfully remark every day on the lack of holy Fear of the Lord in souls, and we become aware of this by the way they receive Confirmation and the other sacraments.

LET US CULTIVATE, *therefore,* the gift of the Fear of the Lord, meditating often on the infinite grandeur of God, on his attributes, and on the power he enjoys over us. Let us consider in the light of faith, the grandeur of the sacraments and, above all, the Eucharist; and let the Fear of the Lord which animates the Church in its rites and in its Liturgy, be mirrored in us. For us, the discipline of the Church is a wonderful schooling in the Fear of the Lord and in the way to treat Jesus. The temple with its splendor, the sacred vestments, the ceremonies, the lights turned on, the tabernacle lamp, the veil of the tabernacle, the silence of the holy place, the majestic solemnity of the chant, the tolling bells, and the sanctuary bell rung at the elevation and at Benediction, all tell us with how much loving reverence and with how much holy fear we must treat Jesus in the Blessed Sacrament and the infinite majesty of God. From this point of view, it is most deplorable to entrust holy things to lay sacristans totally lacking in piety, without any fear of God. Oftentimes, they are known to be notorious sinners, blasphemers, drunkards, and in a word, hirelings or mercenaries, whose conduct damages the wonderful instructions in the Fear of the Lord that the Church imparts to the faithful, as to proper demeanor in the temple.

It is also necessary to cultivate the Fear of the Lord by considering, in the light of faith, what sin is, which however slight it be, is always an offense to God. To arouse this sentiment, it is well to make a careful examination of conscience, stirring up compunction within and humbling oneself before God, meditating on the Passion of Jesus Christ, and uniting with Jesus in His immolation to expiate the sins of men.

It is also necessary to flee all that can generate in us lack of respect for God and for holy things; hence, the need to habituate oneself to exercise good manners and courtesy in treating with God, even in the intimacy of one's own home. To pray stretched out on a bed, for example – except in the case of illness – without bursts of love to prevent or intrude on sleep, out of laziness or simply because it is more comfortable – is absolutely inappropriate, and accustoms one to demonstrate minimal respect for God and holy things. To keep holy icons half hidden in one's home, displaying little or no devotion to them; or to abandon holy relics to the status of dust collectors and other indecorous practices, demonstrates one's lack of respect for God and for holy things, and encourages other household members to do likewise. In such a setting, it becomes very difficult to acquire the gift of the Fear of the Lord which is the beginning of wisdom and order in our lives.

COME, O HOLY Spirit God, fill me with thy holy Fear, that I might live adoring thee with the Father and the Son, the Most Holy Trinity, one God. Come, make me experience a great horror of my faults and a tender love for God, that I might flee accursed sin. Am I not harder than a rock, when I sin with such ease without experiencing remorse for it? Make me sense the magnificence of divine glory, O Holy Spirit God, that overwhelmed by the majesty of God, I might take flight from every fault.

Why am I so insensitive to God and so sensitive to myself? A single act of disdain shown me; a single word addressed to me which I might resent; a single refusal met, causes me more dejection and suffering than a thousand offenses I have done to thy divine Majesty, O my God, Infinite Love! Pour out thy light on me, that I might behold my misery and deliver me from it; soften my heart that I may give it to thee entirely; inflame my will that I might submit it to thine. Create in me a new heart and renew in my inmost self a right spirit, that I might know how to ponder my lowliness and God's grandeur, and live adoring thy majesty in heaven, thy mercy in thy temple, and thine infinite charity – loving thee, Eternal Love. – *Veni, Sancte Spiritus!*

XII. Synthesis of the Gifts of the Holy Spirit from an Admirable Passage in the Works of St. John Baptist Vianney, Curé d'Ars.

The nature, importance, necessity and manner of operating of the gifts of the Holy Spirit in us has been set forth by the holy Curé d'Ars, by this humble, so wise priest though lacking in natural genius, and he did this by means of a gift of the Holy Spirit in such wise as to amaze the world.

His words, replete with limpid simplicity, possess a sweet taste which charms; we believe that they are best suited to grasp the importance of the gifts of the Holy Spirit in our life, and to make us implore them with intense love. Here is the admirable passage which confounds all human wisdom:

Man in himself is nothing, but is much by means of the Holy Spirit. Man is all earthly and animalistic; only the divine Spirit can lift the soul and transport it on high. Why were the saints so detached from earth? Because they allowed themselves to be led by the Holy Spirit. Those led by this divine Spirit have a right concept of everything; and this is why so many unlettered know more than the wise. When one is led by a God in power and in light, one cannot fall into error.

Now the Holy Spirit is power and light. He makes us discern between true and false, and between good and evil. Just as lenses magnify objects, he enables us to see good and evil in bold print. With the Holy Spirit, we see enlarged: the grandeur of the least works of God, and the enormity of the slightest errors. In the same way as the watchmaker examines with his lenses the smallest parts of a watch, so the rays of the Holy Spirit scrutinize in us all the details of our life. Hence, even the slightest sins horrify us. Behold why the Virgin Most Holy never sinned. The Holy Spirit made her grasp the ugliness of evil, and she trembled with fear at the mere thought of the least fall.

Those who possess the Holy Spirit are intolerant of themselves, so well do they know their own misery. The proud are those who lack the Holy Spirit. The worldly do not have the Holy Spirit – or have him only in passing; nor does he remain with them – the noise of the world alienates him. A Christian guided by the Holy Spirit does not experience weariness in abandoning the goods of the world to run after the goods of Heaven, and knows very well how to differentiate between them.

The eye of the world does not see beyond this side of life, just as my eye does not see beyond this wall when the door of the Church is shut. The eye of the Christian sees into the very depths of eternity. To the man who allows himself to be led by the Holy Spirit, he seems not to belong to the world; to the world, he seems not to belong to God... Hence the question is to know who is leading us. If it is not the Holy Spirit, we have much to remedy, for there is neither substance nor savor in anything we do. If it is the Holy Spirit, we experience such tender complacence... as to want to die in peace!

Those who let themselves be led by the Holy Spirit experience every manner of contentment within themselves, while bad Christians roll about amidst thistles and stones. A soul who possesses the Holy Spirit never feels bored in the presence of God; there comes forth from its heart a loving diffusion. Without the Holy Spirit we are like the stone pavement of a street. Pick up in one hand a sponge soaked in water and in the other a cobblestone; squeeze both. From the cobblestone, not a drop comes forth; from the sponge, abundant water escapes. The sponge is the soul filled with the Holy Spirit; the cobblestone is the cold, hard heart, where the Holy Spirit does not dwell.

A soul which possesses the Holy Spirit tastes such savor in prayer, that the time spent, seems all too brief; it never loses the holy presence of God. Its heart, before the divine Crucified or the Sacrament of the Altar, resembles grapes in the wine-press. It is the Holy Spirit who forms thoughts in the hearts of the just, and who speaks their words... Whoever possesses the Holy Spirit, produces nothing evil; all the fruits of the Holy Spirit are good.

Without him, without his seven gifts, everything is cold; hence, when we sense a diminution in our fervor, we must at once make a fervent novena to the Holy Spirit to implore his gifts… Consider for a moment: when one makes a retreat or celebrates a jubilee, one is full of good desires; this is the breath of the Holy Spirit who breathes in our soul and renews all, as does the warm breeze that melts the ice and effects the return of spring… Although you are not great saints, nonetheless, there are moments when you experience the sweetness of prayer and the presence of God; these are visitations of the Holy Spirit. When one possesses this divine Spirit, the heart is opened and immersed in divine love. The fish never complains about too much water; similarly the good Christian never complains about being too long with God. Whoever is bored with Religion, does not possess the Holy Spirit.

If one were to ask the damned: Why are you in hell? – they would reply: for having resisted the Holy Spirit. – And were one to ask the Blessed: Why are you in Heaven? – they would reply: because we listened to the Holy Spirit… – When we have good thoughts, it is the Holy Spirit coming to visit us. The Holy Spirit is power, and by him, St. Simon Stylite was supported on his pillar, and the martyrs were comforted in the circus arena. Without his gifts, even the martyrs would have fallen like leaves from the trees. When the pyres were burning them, the Holy Spirit extinguished the heat of the flames with the warmth of divine love.

In sending us the Holy Spirit, God has treated us like a great monarch who chose one of his ministers to guide a subject, instructing the minister thus: – You will accompany my subject wherever he goes, and bring him back to me safe and sound. – O how lovely, dear children, to be accompanied by the Holy Spirit! He is a good guide… And to say that there are those who do not want to follow him!… The Holy Spirit is like a man who has a good carriage and horse, and who wants to take us to Paris. We have only to say yes and climb aboard… It is very easy to say yes! Well, then, the Holy Spirit wants to take us to Heaven; we have only to say yes, and leave the driving to him.

Here is a rifle in excellent condition. You load it... but you must fire it to hit anything... Similarly we have within us the means to do good... The Holy Spirit reposes in the souls of the just like a dove in its nest. He nurtures good desires in pure souls, as a dove, her chicks. The Holy Spirit leads us as a mother leads her little one by the hand... as a person with sight guides a blind man. The Sacraments instituted by our Lord would not have saved us except for the Holy Spirit. Without him, the very death of our Lord would have been useless to us. And hence, our Lord said to the Apostles: "It is expedient for you that I depart, because if I do not go, the Advocate will not come to you..." [Jn 16: 7] – The descent of the Holy Spirit was necessary to make that harvest of graces ripen. So is it with a grain of wheat: you cast it upon the rich, plowed soil; but sun and rain are still needed to make it sprout, and grow, and send forth ears. Every morning we must say: *Send me the Holy Spirit, O Lord, who will make me know who I am and who thou art.*

The Fruits of the Holy Spirit

＊

I. Fruits of the Holy Spirit: Concept – Nature – Necessity

Our soul cannot save itself and reach eternal glory, if it does not produce supernatural fruits of virtue. John the Baptist said: *Every tree that does not produce good fruit will be cut down and thrown on the fire* [Mt 3: 10]. We are like plants in the vineyard of the Lord and we must bear fruit for him, but we cannot do this except with the grace of the Holy Spirit. From his gifts, and by means of his gifts, fruits mature in us; with the power of germination which he confers on us supernaturally, and with engrafting into Jesus Christ, our soul like a luxuriant plant bears fruit. The fruit, observes St. Thomas, *is the final product of the plant, together with a certain weakness* [*Summa*, I–II, q. 11, a. 1].

The fruit may be wild or domesticated. Wild fruit is the natural fruit of the plant; the domesticated is that which is formed via engrafting of the plant. The graft effects a life within a life, and gives to the plant a strength capable of drawing from the sun more select dispositions and of producing better fruit. We, too, engrafted into Jesus Christ by Baptism [cf. Jn 15: 1 ff] and vivified by the Holy Spirit who, as it were, is the sun which makes us fecund and the water which nourishes us and makes us grow, must bear supernatural fruits.

If we work like men only in human fashion, on the basis of right reason, our actions, even though good from a human point of view, may be compared to wild fruits which in no wise are useful for eternal life, because they have nothing of the divine nature. These actions may be a remote disposition for grace – just as the wild tree bearing good, wild fruits and appearing full of life and luxuriant may more likely be chosen by the farmer for grafting – but the fruits of such actions cannot be genuine means, capable of lifting us to union with God.

If, instead, we work on the basis of sanctifying grace, that is to say: through the merits of Jesus Christ, once we have been engrafted into Him by the Holy Spirit, with the consequent engrafting of the virtues and gifts into us, then our fruits become fruits of divine beauty and goodness, i.e., supernatural fruits of eternal life. These are rightly called *fruits of the Holy Spirit*, because they proceed more from him than from us, and therefore are more his than ours. Hence, we should ascribe the possession to him and the enjoyment to us.

From these first basic concepts, our ideas on true virtue and true perfection of the soul – initially very confused – begin to become clearer. We are easily fascinated by natural virtues, not unknown to pagans, and we believe that the so-called gentleman, the man with the good heart who gives generously; the altruist, committed to the welfare of others; the kindly, courteous man who is incapable of vulgar acts; the true philosopher who, assessing temporal things by right reason, disdains them and detaches himself from them – are truly and supernaturally virtuous. We believe this so strongly, that we prefer such apparent virtues pertaining solely to human nature, to true virtues which are in the profoundest depths of the soul, sprouting only by means of God's grace. At times we look upon naturally virtuous persons – trees full of wild fruit – with greater sympathy than persons whose virtue is based on grace – who are engrafted trees – the fruit of which, in virtue of human frailty and misery, may also be extremely damaged – yet, in spite of that, ever remaining sweet, ripe, and healthy fruit for the life of the soul.

We are ever surprised at the natural virtue of people without faith, as an unskilled farmer is amazed to see a wild plant full of fruit; and we remain scandalized by the defects and faults we observe in virtuous Catholics, because we esteem that latter tree to be good and would like to see it entirely perfect. The admiration for good infidels, at root, derives from the fact that we do not expect fruit from wild trees; and the disappointment over imperfect believers comes from the fact that we do not expect rotten fruit from those engrafted trees flourishing in fertile and luxuriant soil. Meanwhile, fascination for naturally virtuous non-believers is a real danger, because it can lead us to adopt their ideas and style of living, *and detach ourselves from true life*. For this reason it is supremely important to form for ourselves a precise notion of the fruits of the Holy Spirit; and we insist on this, so that Christian life, engrafted in Jesus Christ and animated by the Holy Spirit, be supernaturally and totally virtuous and holy.

The soul which faithfully corresponds with the actual graces God gives it and puts in action the infused virtues received in Baptism, and the gifts of the Holy Spirit received in Confirmation, produces *acts* of virtue, imperfect and tiring at first, in reaction to the opposition of its own corrupt nature; later, better and more gratifying with the increase of grace and the activity of the gifts of the Holy Spirit which the exercise of virtue obtains from God. These fruits are like the ripening of the first acts of virtue – at first, still immature and sour fruits – afterwards, leaving the soul with profound joy and pleasure, as it were, in the tasting of ripened fruit; thus constituting *the gifts of the Holy Spirit*, which can, therefore, be defined as: *virtuous acts which have attained a certain degree of perfection, and which fill the soul with joy*.

The fruits are distinguished from the infused virtues and from the gifts, as an action is distinguished from a power to act. In fact, the fruits are not powers inhering in the soul, but are acts, *actions*, deriving from the holy habits which the Holy Spirit gives to the soul.

Not all acts of virtue, however, merit the name of *fruits*, but only those accompanied by a certain spiritual sweetness.

This spiritual sweetness pervades the soul when, with the grace of the Holy Spirit and the docility which this gives, the soul performs an act of virtue with love and generosity. If the soul performs this imperfectly, whether by failing to correspond to the interior promptings of grace, or by performing an act of virtue out of a mixture of human and natural motives, such an action may be regarded as good in view of human frailty, but in no wise can it be defined *a fruit of the Holy Spirit* in the proper sense of this word.

The highest degree of perfection of the fruits consists in the *beatitudes*, or in the heroism of the fundamental virtues at the level of a life totally supernaturalized; the beatitudes then are the prelude to eternal life.

It is not a matter of indifference for us, nor a simple act of supererogation to produce the fruits of the Holy Spirit, for if we do not produce these fruits, we shall produce those of the flesh. If we do not produce fruits of eternal life, we shall produce the fruits of eternal death. There is no in-between state. Indeed, Jesus Christ compares us to branches on a vine, and demands that they bear fruit. Jesus says: *I am the true vine, and my Father is the vine-dresser; every branch in me which does not bear fruit, he will take away, and every branch which bears fruit he will cleanse, so that it bear more fruit... Abide in me and I in you; as the branch cannot bear fruit of itself, unless it remain on the vine, so neither can you bear fruit unless you abide in me... because without me you can do nothing* [Jn 15: 1–5].

Jesus condemned the sterile fig tree, on which he found nothing but leaves and, at His curse, the fig tree immediately withered [cf. Mt 21: 19]. He demands from us, then, fruits in proportion to the graces which we have received. He comes to observe our soul as he observed the fig tree, and if He finds leaves of apparent virtues wanting in true fruits, He can say to us with reason: – With Baptism I have given you innocence, and where in you is the fruit of that virtue which the Holy Spirit has poured out into you? I have given you the Holy

Spirit himself that you might have lived in justice, and these fruits of justice, where are they? I have filled your soul with the grace of contrition, that you might repent, and where are the fruits of repentance? [cf. Mt 3: 8]. I have made you know my love, and where is the correspondence of your love with mine, where is your generosity? [cf. Mt 10: 8]. On your soul I have showered treasures of mercy, and where are the fruits of such mercy in you? [cf. Mt 5: 7]. – How necessary, then, to consider the fruits of the Holy Spirit and implore them of God that he produce them in us and make them ripen according to the designs of his love and of his charity in our life.

II. Listing of the Fruits of the Holy Spirit – Summary of Their Meaning and of Their Value – Order of Listing

God has placed a very great variety among the fruits which the earth produces. The diversity, in fact, of fruits in various regions, in various climates, and even in very limited rural areas is surprising. Now what happens in the field, occurs also in the spirit, for the fruits of the Holy Spirit are as many as there are acts of virtue which can sprout from the virtues and the gifts of the Holy Spirit.

These fruits are nuanced in their diversity: according to the particular dispositions of the souls in which they mature, precisely as certain kinds of fruit flourish more in one land rather than another. Strictly speaking, therefore, it is difficult, if not impossible, to make a complete listing. Nonetheless, Scripture and the Church agree on a list of twelve principal fruits of the Holy Spirit. St. Paul lists them in this way in his letter to the Galatians, according to the *Vulgate* text, by contrasting them with the accursed works of the flesh.

Here is the text of the Apostle: *Now the works of the flesh are manifest, which are immorality, uncleanness, licentiousness, idolatry, witchcrafts, enmities, contentions, jealousies, anger, quarrels, factions, parties, envies, murders, drunkenness, carousings, and such like... But the* fruits of the Spirit are:

charity, joy, peace, patience, kindness, goodness, longsuffering, gentleness, faith, modesty, continence, chastity [Gal 5: 19–23; cf. Rom 8: 1–38].

A first glance at the ensemble of these fruits shows that the first three: charity, joy, peace, regard the soul's relations with God himself: *charity* is the love which unites us to God; *joy* is the gratitude and thanks for the infinite divine goodness in which we live and move [cf. Acts 17: 28]; *peace* is tranquil rest in God, secure in the order of his Law, and hence, it is tranquility in our inmost self and with our neighbor.

Next follow the fruits, which individually and specifically regard one's neighbor, the first being *patience*. Do we bear with our neighbor, or are we irritable, vindictive, resentful and malicious? If it is the latter, we are far from the *kindness* of God. From a good heart as from a pure fountain comes forth *goodness* [cf. Mt 7: 15–20]; but goodness which is a fruit of the Holy Spirit is not a simple, naturally good heart in virtue of the sensibility of its nerves and organs; it is the supernaturally good heart which comes from the love of God above all things and in all creatures.

Longsuffering is the perennial radiation of a loving heart, that treats everyone lovingly and judges their defects with kindness; it is a more generous charity toward one's neighbor, more constant and persevering in doing good.

Gentleness is affectionate, kind, tolerant, dismisses injuries and resentment, sincere in loving kindness, without harboring in one's heart, grudges against others. *Faith* [fidelity] is the observance and maintenance of a pledged word, not for motives of human respect, but for love of God, because one considers his pledged word as an oath.

Finally, there are the fruits which refer to ourselves: *modesty* – in one's comportment, conduct, attire, in dealings with others and not meddling in their affairs, and in delicate thoughtfulness of all; *continence* – by means of which we repress disorderly passions: anger, indulgence of pleasures, ambition for honors, etc.; lastly, *chastity* – the transparent purity of soul, the custody of the senses, and the renunciation of all that might give occasion for staining the soul.

Before explaining in detail, let us now review in summary fashion, the significance and value of these twelve fruits in our soul, to facilitate our remembrance of them:

1) Charity consists in loving God and neighbor. *2) Joy* arises out of this love, and transcends all the joys of this world. *3) Peace* results from our submission to God and from our union with our neighbor. *4) Patience* makes us bear any adversity for love of God. *5) Kindness* inclines us to treat our neighbor with affability and courtesy, even if our enemy. *6) Goodness* inclines us to do good to all without discrimination. *7) Longsuffering* makes us persevere in patience, making us open-handed and generous with all. *8) Gentleness* makes us indulgent with the weaknesses of our neighbor, restrains our anger, and makes us bear calmly the privations of life. *9) Faith* makes us keep our word and avoid all suspicion, hypocrisy, and deception. *10) Modesty* makes us compose our outer appearance, and control our actions so as to edify others. *11) Continence* makes us abstain even from legitimate pleasures, and keep within proper limits our exterior and interior sentiments. *12) Chastity* makes us repress disorderly desires of the flesh, and makes us preserve purity of soul.

These fruits are not synonymous with the virtues implied in them, but are their acts. Thus we may say that *we perform a charity* when we offer to help our neighbor, when in reality we perform *an act of charity*. We have said that the order of these fruits regards God, our neighbor and ourselves; we may add, following St. Thomas, that the order of their listing, reflects the identical way in which the Holy Spirit deals with man. He leads man, step by step, to perfection and to the happiness which derives from it, orientating him toward

God with *charity, joy and peace*; ordering him in himself with *patience, kindness and goodness*; orientating him toward his neighbor with *longsuffering, gentleness and faith*; making him control what is disordered by means of *modesty, continence and chastity*.

III. Detailed Explanation of Each Fruit of the Holy Spirit

1) Charity – Charity is the first fruit of the Holy Spirit, foundation and root of all the others. Being himself infinite Charity, or infinite Love, it is logical that he should communicate to the soul his flame, making the soul love God with its whole heart, with all its strength and with all its mind, and its neighbor for love of God. Where this love is wanting, there can be found no supernatural act, no merit of eternal life, no true and complete happiness. It is logical also, that charity be a most sweet fruit, because the love of God is the attainment of one's proper end on earth and is the principle of its attainment in eternity; hence, it is the full satisfaction of one's entire being. In speaking specifically of *charity*, then, it is clear that one does not intend to speak of the virtue of *kindness*, although this is included in *charity* as a particular manifestation and outpouring of love toward one's neighbor.

Charity, fruit of the Holy Spirit, is principally the flame of love for God, esteem for him above all things; tender respect for his majesty, adoration of him in the Trinity; affectionate care in honoring him and making him honored; generous detachment from all to find him, the treasure of the soul, the power of love which makes one conquer every obstacle blocking the exercise of the virtues, which makes one take up and carry one's cross as a treasure, and which makes however much one does for God always seem very little.

From this flame of charity is born that of the love of neighbor, but this love is not natural tenderness and compassion toward one suffering; it is not prodigality in giving to one who is in need, but is *love of God in his image*, a love a thousand times more beneficial to one's neighbor who suffers, because it is not motivated by sympathy for others or by personal need to be generous, but is given out of esteem for God. Hence, it is steady, impartial, and heroic in its every manifestation, and possesses the highest value even in its least outpouring, because charity is the admirable alchemy which can change rocks into precious gold.

2) Joy – It is a fruit which spontaneously arises from charity as fragrance from a flower, light from the sun, heat from fire. Every good work done with ease gives to the soul a profound joy, an effect of the satisfaction which one has in the victory won over self and in having produced good. In charity, then, joy surpasses all measure, because to our love corresponds the love of God. The soul not only enjoys a calm, holy conscience free of all anxiety, but is replete with joy from the love of God which overflows in the soul in response to that soul's love.

The joy which comes from the Holy Spirit does not grow dim even in tribulations. During those times, this joy can increase when tribulations are testimony to the love of God, as St. Paul could exclaim: *I overflow with joy in all our troubles* [II Cor 7: 4].

The joy of the Holy Spirit is very different from what the world claims to offer in its diversions. *Impure sensual delight*, says St. John Chrysostom [Homily 13 on Acts], *is similar to the sensual pleasure which the scabrous feel when they scratch themselves, because after the brief pleasure there follows a much longer pain and a still more bothersome annoyance.* The sensuous pleasure of the world is slavery; the joy of the Holy Spirit is freedom of the spirit and freedom from matter; the soul breathes in the atmosphere of the divine, and experiences the joy of one who emerges from a cellar into the sun light, or escapes from tumultuous waves to the security of solid ground.

3) Peace – True joy, without the turmoil that divided love engenders – brings with it the peace which is its perfection, because it supports and guarantees the tranquil enjoyment of the object loved. For the soul, the loved object *par excellence* can only be God, and hence, peace is the tranquil security of possessing him and of being in his grace. This is the peace of the Lord *which surpasses all understanding*, as St. Paul says [Phil 4: 7], because it is a profound joy surpassing every joy based on the flesh or on material things, and to attain this, we must immolate everything to God.

4) Patience – Life being a continuous warfare against enemies visible and invisible, and against the powers of the world and of hell [cf. Eph 6: 10–17], much patience is required to overcome the disturbance such struggles produce in us, and to find ourselves in harmony with the creatures with whom we must deal – so diverse in character, education, aspirations, and often dominated by fixations of every kind. There exists a natural patience which makes us put up with adversity via diplomacy, opportunism, prudence of the flesh, or because such things are inevitable and invincible; and there is the patience which makes us bear adversity simply for the love of God or out of profound charity for our neighbor.

A condemned man, for example, finds himself face-to-face with the inevitable, and bears with the consequences of condemnation with a certain fatalism which gives him no peace, but does permit him a gloomy, dark, and painful calm. A poor man, made aware of the injustices of another, and who is pervaded and sustained by the grace of the Holy Spirit, suffers quietly for the love of God. Uniting himself affectionately to the Passion to Jesus Christ, he looks forward to eternal glory. He considers how God is pleased with his suffering and with the forgiveness he extends to those who offend him; and he not only feels the strength to bear with adversity, but experiences in the very depths of his soul, a soothing sweetness, fruit of a greater union with God, gained from his encounter with human misery and the delusions with which creatures fill him.

In humiliations, the soul enters a profound interior silence, when on being demeaned by men the soul abases itself before God; during injury the soul feels itself broken in spirit, remains like Jesus amidst the mockery of His Passion, and experiences an ineffable sweetness in pondering how God alone is the judge who will pass sentence on it. In adversities, it becomes recollected in the gentle arms of God's providence and rejoices in believing with firm hope that God will take care of all. The tempest roars about, yet it is neither disturbed nor suffers because of it. Rather, it sails with Jesus Christ in the stern of the battered boat, awakens Him with the most affectionate prayers, and has faith that when He arises, He will calm the storm as He did on the lake [cf. Mt 8:23–27].

The multiple facets of patience, are fruits of habitual grace which confer on us a serene, supernatural character of actual grace, which moves us to accept suffering for the love of God; of faith, which makes us see God in everything; of hope, causing us to abandon all to him; of charity, compelling us to love him with all our heart; of justice, urging us to acknowledge ourselves as sinners in need of every means of atonement; of fortitude, which keeps us steady in adversity and sustains us in bearing with it; of prudence, prompting us to avoid confrontations and quarrels; and of temperance which moderates and restrains any reactions that we might have. From these strong roots, the flower of patience blossoms by means of the Holy Spirit, and ripens as the sweetest fruit of charity and peace.

5) Kindness – Patience finds its perfection in kindness or in the constant disposition to leniency, and to affability in conversation in responding and in doing good.

One can be good and generous without being *kind*, indulging a rude, ill-mannered and harsh behavior in one's dealings; kindness makes one sociable, civil, and pleasant in speech and in comportment, notwithstanding the rudeness, bad manners, and harshness of others. It is a great sign of holiness of a soul, and of the action of the Holy Spirit in it, who, as the Book of Wisdom says [7: 22–23] *is the spirit of understanding: holy, one, manifold, subtle, eloquent, active, undefiled, sure, sweet, loving that which is good; perceptive, quick, which nothing hindereth; beneficent, gentle, kind, steadfast, assured, secure.*

The kind soul is *intelligent,* because that soul considers things and persons with discerning equity, and is neither irked nor irksome; softens the sharp edges, as they say, and rounds them off so as to leave in itself only an affectionate sympathy, a graciousness and a simple, spontaneous, delicate, and modestly outgoing courtesy.

The kind soul is *holy,* because such a soul loves God alone and acts out of love for him; is *one,* because that soul is wholly for each person; is *manifold,* because it is wholly for all; is *subtle,* because that soul penetrates to the bottom of hearts with its sweet charm; is *eloquent,* because it is so moving in its speech; is *active,* because it gives with generosity; is *undefiled,* because it has no hidden agenda in what it does, and is most pure in its affections.

The kind soul is *sure* (infallible), not because it cannot err, but because such a soul keeps to the point in dealing with others, integrating character and conciliating opponents; the kind soul is *sweet,* does not allow itself to be upset by shocks and disappointments which persons can provoke. The kind soul is *loving of that which is good* because it seeks only what is good; is perceptive and quick in delicate affection which nothing hindereth; is *beneficent* with charity; is *loving of persons* whom it considers its brethren and children; is *kind,* therefore, *steadfastly* kind, *assured* and *tranquil* in all that it does for others. All this is a transfusion of true holiness which the Holy Spirit gave that soul, and hence, people measure a soul's sanctity by its kindness, thereby having subjected itself to be drawn, captivated, enveloped, and ruled by it.

6) Goodness – Goodness is the kindly affection which one has in doing good to one's neighbor, and is the fruit of kindness, as it were, for one who suffers and is in need of help. Kindness itself, gives to goodness a perfume, a warmth, a savor of the fruit. Goodness is kindness in action. Goodness, infinite goodness – effect of the soul's union with God – is poured out by the Christian soul upon its neighbor, benefitting and healing, in imitation of Jesus Christ. Goodness, bestowing benefactions with love, is the characteristic note on which St. Peter announces Jesus Christ to the centurion, Cornelius, and those gathered with him. St. Peter says: *You know... how God anointed Jesus of Nazareth with the Holy Spirit and with power, and he went about doing good and healing all...* [Acts 10: 37–38].

The life of Jesus Christ on this earth was totally taken up in doing good to others, thus showing a Heart replete with affection and goodness. He made all mankind feel the vibrations and pulsations of His most tender Heart bequeathed to the Church, His Mystical Body. There is no work of charity in the Christian world, of which the Sacred Heart is not the shining principle, animating and vivifying it. Before His coming, the world with its culture and activities, was as cold as ice, as hard as rock, as cruel as beasts; the Sacred Heart of Jesus warmed it with His loving goodness, and sent the fire of His love into the souls of the Apostles, that in proclaiming the Gospel they might be ministers of His charity.

The Church, from the times of the Apostles to the present, has not done other than pour out in works of beneficence and charity, the infinite goodness of Jesus Christ; and the saints have been, through Jesus and with Jesus, the most blessed of beings, precisely in virtue of the goodness poured forth in them by the Holy Spirit. We, too, as members of the Mystical Body of Jesus Christ, must possess this goodness; and we must also have it both in the apostolate and in private life, thus confounding the arrogance of those who pretend to be friends of the people, but drag them into ruin, robbing them of faith and leaving them prey to disorders and seditions. The hypocritical goodness of these perverts is not a fruit of the Holy Spirit, but of a diabolical spirit, using some temporal benefit as bait to captivate souls and destroy them eternally.

7) Longsuffering – This fruit of the Holy Spirit confers on the soul a breadth of vision and generosity, whereby, on encountering delay in the realization of its plans, the soul knows how to await the moments of Divine Providence, and how to practice goodness and patience with one's neighbor, without becoming weary from resistance and opposition. *Longsuffering* is the same thing as long-lasting courage or longanimity: *longus animus*, in difficulties strewed in the path of good, and largesse of mind: *magnificentia*, supernatural largesse, in the conception and in the execution of works of goodness.

A person is not *longsuffering* who is mean, stingy, petty, short on confidence in God, and whose hand is paralyzed – indeed, we might even say, frozen solid – when there is question of charity for his neighbor. He is not longsuffering who sees everything from a black, cynical, dismal, distorted point of view; and does not reconcile with, compassionate, console, and succor his neighbor at the opportune moment. He is longsuffering, who does not trust in himself, but confides in God; he is not anxious, but abandons himself to God and does not cease to do good, ever going forward, not relying on his own powers, but on the help of divine grace.

8) Gentleness – In the commentary on the letters of St. Paul for many centuries ascribed to St. Anselm,[11] a person is defined as gentle *who adapts to others, who is tractable, docile, flexible, easy to get along with, calm in suffering*. Gentleness is opposed to anger and animosity – anger in reacting, and animosity in not wanting to suffer, in not bearing with the domination or imposition of others – vindicating injuries received and exonerating the most contemptible assaults. Gentleness makes

---

11   This commentary is now acknowledged to be the work of Hervé of Bordeaux (12th century).

the Christian a dove without bitterness, a lamb without anger, all sweetness poured out in speech and in conduct, in the face of another's rage.

Like Jesus, who was the meekest of lambs, and who invited us to learn this virtue from Him: *Learn of me who am meek and humble of heart* [Mt 11: 29], the Christian *does not break the broken reed, nor extinguish the smoldering wick* [Mt 12: 20]. The Christian who is gentle conquers and controls his disorderly nerves, the enemies of this great virtue, and cause whereby the soul is caught up in quarrels and dissension.

Nervous reaction can also be a fruit of misfortune, of uncontrolled excitement, which can leave one in a momentary state of insanity. But when the soul possesses the sweet fruit of gentleness, and implores it incessantly in prayer from the Holy Spirit, then it experiences ease in controlling these senseless, nervous explosions, and can reach a point of experiencing a great taste for putting up with annoying persons out of love for God and conforming oneself to Jesus Christ.

Meekness is a fruit which has need of cultivation, habituating oneself not to act explosively even when obstacles are met in material work; with one's neighbor humility, sympathy and patience are needed. He who gets accustomed to huffing and puffing when the needle will not thread, when the button comes off one's dress, when the shoe lace breaks, when the key does not open, when the catarrh annoys, when the cough torments, when the fever drives one crazy, and for similar personal upsets – such a person does not even notice how he indulges the gymnastic of irritability, and so falls into the habit of exploding against his neighbor. It is necessary to practice just the contrary gymnastic, and by patience with material things, open one's heart to the Holy Spirit that he might fill it with sweetness and gentleness.

9) Faith – By many, this is also called *fidelity*, so making clear that the theological virtue of faith is not denoted by this fruit, but is to be understood in the sense of *fidelity*. St. Anselm defines it thus: *Faith is veracity (truth-keeping) in promises*, the exact contrary to fraud and lying. Consequently, this fruit of the Holy Spirit makes us maintain our pledged word, assumed tasks, and agreed-upon contracts; moreover, in respect to our neighbor, it keeps us from being suspicious, evil-minded, incredulous of anything he says, insincere, manipulative, and betraying. This faith is the soul of any human association, industry, commerce, and of all civilization.

Keeping one's pledged word, as well as being prompt in meeting appointments and observing prescribed schedules, is a virtue which glorifies God as truth. One who makes an appointment and then arrives late; who promises and then fails to deliver; who honors a person in his presence and then despises him behind his back – is wanting in that dove-like simplicity recommended to us by Jesus Christ [cf. Mt. 10:16], and influences others to be suspicious about social relationships of any kind. These intrigues, sadly characteristic of modern life, are nothing other than total deception and diametrically opposed to this fruit of the Holy Spirit. Hence, it is necessary to habituate oneself to straightforwardness and simplicity, without excluding the prudence of the serpent, inseparable complement of this virtue, also insinuated and taught by Jesus Himself [cf. Mt 10: 16].

10) Modesty – This is a virtue which orders and properly disposes our exterior being, i.e., all our members placed by God at the service of the soul, in such wise that they reflect, as much as possible, the internal order and spiritual beauty of the soul. Modesty, as the name indicates, *sets the mode* (in the sense of norms for good behavior) i.e., regulates the pleasing and dignified manner of dressing, of walking, of speaking, of laughing, of playing. As the reflex of a calm interior, it moderates our eyes lest they wander to foolish and filthy things, so reflecting in them the purity of the soul; forms our lips to display a smile of simplicity and charity in harmony with gestures that embrace all that is gracious and refined.

Etiquette and good manners which every Christian, including the unschooled, should cultivate, comprise a part of modesty because modesty moderates the entire state and all the actions of a civil person and has its foundation in charity. *The attire of the body*, the Holy Spirit tells us, *and the laughter of the teeth, and the gait of the man, show us what he is* [Eccles 19: 27]. And Hervé of Bordeaux (12th century), in his commentary on the letters of St. Paul, for many centuries formerly ascribed to St. Anselm, describes all this divinely: *From his external actions, one can assess the inner man hidden in one's heart, if he be fickle, if he be proud, if he be troubled, if he be serious, constant, pure and mature* [I *Offic.* 18]. Hence, St. Augustine in his *Rule* [no. 3] states: *Let there be nothing in your actions which might offend the glance of anyone, but be such as are befitting your sanctity.*

Modesty, then, is not an act of hypocrisy, but a fruit of interior holiness; it is not practiced to be considered saints, but to make resplendent the light of good example for the edification of all, glorifying the Father who is in Heaven [cf. Mt 5: 14–16]. It is not only an external manifestation of composure, as it were an ostentation of one's own excellence, but rather includes a profound sentiment of humility which is contrary to every kind of ostentation, and which tends to hide in a simple and honest reserve any good qualities, attainments or excellence a person might possess.

Jesus Christ is our model in regard to this precious virtue, which confers a sweet charm on perfection, and induces in others, esteem and the desire for what is good. For this reason St. Paul wished that the modesty of Christians be known throughout the whole world, considering that this would contribute to its conversion [cf. Phil 4: 5]. For this reason, God has surrounded and ever continues to surround his saints with this halo of spiritual charm, which makes them apostles and promoters of good. In the face and in the comportment of saints, one reads holiness; and their modesty is the halo of light which makes them known to the world, to its edification.

11) Continence – The exterior of a man is kept in order by modesty; modesty is not a true virtue if its foundation is not in a man's interior, and if it is not a reflection of a moderated life (measured, regular, according to a rule). Continence keeps the interior man in order, and as the name indicates, *contains* concupiscence within appropriate limits, not only as regards sensual pleasures, but also those related to eating, drinking, entertainment, and other pleasures of material life. The satisfaction of all these instincts, which likens a man to animals, is set in order by continence; and by means of continence which has as goal and motive the love of God, man comes to be spiritualized and sublimated. This control of the lower tendencies of nature, whose disorder seems to constitute the source of an irresistible impetus, is the exclusive glory of the Christian, and is the most evident sign of the presence of the Holy Spirit in him. It is written in the Book of Wisdom, ch. 8: 21, that *no one can be continent*, except God give it and the soul beseech him for this gift.

In a narrower and more particular sense, by *continence* is meant the inner struggle by which, with the grace of God, one achieves control over the impure passions as mentioned in the above-cited commentary of Hervé. It is a fruit of the Holy Spirit which changes men into angels, because in giving them the strength to resist the charm of sensual pleasures, it brings them to the peace of purity; in reality there is nothing so stupid as pleasure of the flesh, because it is a pleasure which gives nothing. It consumes the energies of life, overturns the order of the organism, is the cause of dangerous illness, dulls the mind, brutalizes the heart, renders men supreme egoists, and can lead to every kind of sin. The more impurity dominates a creature, the more it makes him slave to scandalous behavior, entertaining himself in the mire and living in a most filthy manner.

The man who gives himself over to impurity, throws himself into an abyss of evils, degrading himself, losing his peace and the grace of God, to gain but a momentary and shameful delight, which is immediately transformed into the most bitter of delusions and burning remorse. If a man would think but a moment on this, he would find the strength to resist the charm of the senses, just as he discovers, when for the sake of his health, under orders from his physician, he abstains from smoking, from wine and from those foods to which his gluttony is most solicitous. But in the area of impurity, man feels himself dragged along, because the world and the devil tempt him in every possible way, and because he himself seeks out occasions of sin and puts himself in proximate and irresistible danger of falling.

On the other hand, if one abstains from impurity only out of human motives such as personal advantage and opportunism, such a man's virtue would not be worthy of eternal reward. Man, then, has need of the grace of the Holy Spirit. Transforming the carnal man into the spiritual; that grace confers on him a love for tending to God alone, and with pleasant joy, the ability to overcome the forceful demands of the senses, giving him moderation and sobriety in the use of legitimate marriage, and making predominant in him the holy desire of giving God children to serve him, to love him and to gain everlasting life.

12) Chastity – Continence consists in struggle, writes the above-cited author, *and chastity consists in peace.* Chastity is the victory won over the flesh which makes the Christian a living temple of the Holy Spirit. The chaste soul, whether virginal or married (for chastity is not only virginal but spousal, and consists in the perfect order and use of marriage) rules over its body in great peace, and feels in itself the ineffable joy of intimate friendship with God. Jesus himself said: *Blessed are the pure of heart, for they shall see God* [Mt 5: 8].

The Christian who lives chastely, especially a virgin and all consecrated to God, establishes respect on earth, forms the delight of the heavens, and is the beloved temple of the Holy Spirit. His appearance is serene, his look limpid, his speech most pleasing for its purity, his company delightful because it exudes the odor of goodness and amiability. He is a soul in which the Holy Spirit can work freely because, concupiscence being chained, all the other passions are fairly easily brought under control; he is a soul, therefore, who can rise to great holiness, and whose voice in prayer penetrates the heavens and is heard more readily by God.

The Holy Spirit chisels such a soul, enriches it, adorns it with gems, opens to it vast horizons of contemplation, makes use of it in the holy works of the Church, and can enrich it with his *charisms*, of which we will speak later on. In the chaste soul, the Holy Spirit completes his wonderful work of elevating a man to God, and of making him a sharer in the divine nature; this is the final result of his grace, of his gifts, of his fruits. Amazing contrast! The devil, persuading Eve to partake of the forbidden fruit to offer it to Adam, promised her that in eating it, she would become similar to God; instead, falling into sin, they became ever more like the beasts [cf. Gen 3: 1–8]. The Holy Spirit also offers his fruits to man with the same promise, and by means of them, man truly attains to a share in the divine nature.

IV. Fruits of the Holy Spirit Contrasted With the Works of the Flesh

St. Paul, as we have said, in enumerating the twelve fruits of the Holy Spirit, contrasts them with those called *works of the flesh*, of which he gives us a list, cited above. It is not a complete list, but only a vast exemplification, just as the list of the fruits of the Holy Spirit is incomplete, even in the context of the Apostle. Flesh, in the language of theology, is a synonym for *polluted concupiscence, or degraded nature; works of the flesh* are mortal sins which derive from concupiscence, and which degrade man in the horrors of the passions, maximally in those of impurity.

They are said to be *works* of the flesh and not *fruits*, because they are not the seeds of life, but are its corruption; living plants bear fruit, but those cut down dry out and rot. Corruption, therefore, is not a fruit but a vitiating operation, not natural, but contrary to right reason and to the laws of God.

The first work of the flesh listed by the Apostle is *impurity*: *fornication* in its various manifestations, or the complete and consummated sin. This degrading act is opposed to charity, which is love for God and for neighbor, because impurity concentrates the soul on the material which is maximally degrading and maximally separating from God; tends to use one's neighbor to satisfy one's most disordered instincts, and disturbs a human being to his very depths, thus drying up the other fruits of the Holy Spirit which are *joy* of the heart, *chastity* of the spirit, *modesty* of the senses, and *peace* of the soul. The sin of impurity is in itself an *idolatry* of the flesh and of the creature, as idolatry was a disgraceful exercise of impure rites, and is contrary to charity because opposed to God himself, whose glory it robs, and to one's neighbor, whose nobility it degrades.

Witchcrafts, enmities, contentions, jealousies, are opposed to *patience, kindness, goodness and longsuffering.* So, also, *anger and quarrels* – opposed to *gentleness* – foment *factions*, ignite *envies* and provoke *murders* by way of bloody feuds which rise up among peoples, families and individuals. *Drunkenness and carousing* are opposed to *continence*, as also the disintegration of the senses produced by drunkenness and carousing.

Further, all the works of the flesh are opposed to the *faith* owed to God and due to men as well. The carnal man lives for the works of the flesh, and the spiritual man, for the works of the Holy Spirit. It is necessary, therefore, to mortify every filthy and disordered desire, and live by loving God above all things, and desiring eternal glory.

The Beatitudes

♋

I. The Beatitudes: Their Nature – Concepts – Ascending Order: Virtues, Gifts, Beatitudes – Harmony of Reward With Each Beatitude – Incremental Order

When Jesus Christ began His public ministry and saw how great a crowd was following Him, He went up a mountain, and after He was seated, began to teach them, pronouncing a discourse which has rightly been regarded as the basic codification of all His doctrine. He spoke thus: – *Blessed are the poor in spirit, for theirs is the kingdom of heaven. – Blessed are the meek, for they shall possess the earth. – Blessed are they who mourn, for they shall be comforted. – Blessed are they who hunger and thirst for justice, for they shall be satisfied. – Blessed are the merciful, for they shall obtain mercy. – Blessed are the pure of heart, for they shall see God. – Blessed are the peacemakers, for they shall be called the children of God. – Blessed are they who suffer persecution for justice' sake, for theirs is the kingdom of heaven. Blessed are you when men reproach you, and persecute you, and, speaking falsely, say all manner of evil against you, for my sake. Rejoice and exult, because your reward is great in heaven for so did they persecute the prophets who were before you.* [Mt 5: 3–12].

These teachings in eight articles, so to say, each beginning with the word: *Blessed*, are called the *Eight Beatitudes*. They are not simple declarations, but reveal eight active states of perfection at work in the soul and represent the final crown in the work of God in us. These states are also fruits of the Holy Spirit, but mature fruits, so perfect that they give us a foretaste of heavenly blessedness while still in this vale of tears

117

and amidst the harshest trials of life. The beatitudes, therefore, represent the heroism of the virtues, and the action in us, higher than the gifts of the Holy Spirit, and as the theologians say, may be considered thus: *the gifts of the Holy Spirit in action.*

Every fruit of the Holy Spirit requires and presupposes a renunciation made out of love, and by means of this, confers a savory delight in the soul; every beatitude requires a heroism of complete self-denial, and on this condition, renders the soul blessed in full freedom and in full union with God, and prepares it for eternal blessedness. To achieve this renunciation and to taste this freedom in the love of God, the soul has need of a special outpouring in it of the gifts of the Holy Spirit. Consequently, the gifts are to the beatitudes as causes to effects, the spring to the river, trees to flower and fruit, faculties in capacity to act to faculties acting in fact.

Among the moral virtues, the gifts and beatitudes exist in ascending order or order based on degree of perfection.

Virtue, for example, induces a man to make use of honors and riches in moderation; the gifts make him disdain these excesses, allowing him greater freedom and independence from earthly goods; the beatitudes leave him completely detached – a detachment, first borne interiorly – which may rise to the ideal of voluntary poverty: *Blessed are the poor in spirit.*

Virtue moderates and restrains outbursts of anger; the gift makes it easy for the soul to accept suffering and grant pardon; the beatitude establishes an inalterable state of meekness in the soul which draws all hearts to itself: *Blessed are the meek.*

Virtue, accompanied by strained effort or resignation, makes us put up grudgingly with the privations of life; the gift unites us to the Divine Will in loving submission; the beatitude enables us to appreciate suffering as source of eternal riches and as testimony to the love of God, making us even yearn and long for it in intimate and savory delight: *Blessed are those who mourn.*

Virtue makes us practice justice, giving to others their due; the gift makes us generous in carrying out this duty; the beatitude makes us desire more the advantage of others than our own, detaching us from the interests of life: *Blessed are those who hunger and thirst for justice.*

Virtue makes us practice charity toward our neighbor out of compassion, since it makes us regard our neighbor as an image of God; the gift makes us forget ourselves and makes us console others to give pleasure to God; the beatitude confers on us a maternal tenderness for all – believers and non-believers, those nearby and those far away, the just and sinners, friends and enemies – and opens the soul to the mercy which is inspired by Jesus, pardoning and loving: *Blessed are the merciful.*

Virtue makes us exercise purity by struggling; the gift makes us desire and practice it by loving it; the beatitude makes us gives ourselves wholly to God in renouncing the legitimate pleasures of life, and unites us to him alone with all our heart, in thought, intentions, desires, and actions: *Blessed are the pure of heart.*

Virtue makes us remain at peace with all, bearing with the weaknesses of others; the gift makes us keep peace and share peace with the openheartedness of charity and of pleasantness; the beatitude makes us foster peace in families and in the world, desiring to unite all in charity as children of God: *Blessed are the peacemakers.*

Virtue makes us tolerate contradictions with patience; the gift makes us tolerate the same with the generosity of pardon and of peace; the beatitude makes us desire martyrdom: *Blessed are those who suffer persecution for justice' sake.*

It is by reason of this heroic desire for martyrdom, and of the heroic suffering experienced in encountering persecutions and the harm done by the perverse, that Jesus adds to this beatitude: *Blessed are you when men reproach you, and persecute you, and speaking falsely, say all manner of evil against you, for my sake. Rejoice and exult, because your reward is great in heaven; for so did they persecute the prophets who went before you.*

On earth, the beatitudes give the happiness of full freedom of the spirit and of union with God. In this poor world, in fact, there is no other true freedom of the spirit. The *poor in spirit* possess the kingdom of Heaven which is within them; the *meek* possess the earth, or the creatures that dwell upon it and that are submissive to them by the power of their delightfulness. *Those who mourn* are consoled, both by the grace of God and by the charity of the good. *Those who hunger and thirst for justice,* longing to see it triumph, are *satisfied,* because they discern its realization in the events of history. *The merciful* are happy *to find mercy* with God and neighbor. *The pure of heart* overcome the suffocating smog of the flesh and *see God* in themselves, whether in the illuminations of grace or the interior joy which gives them assurance of being with God. *The peacemakers* experience themselves as children of God in the true, universal brotherhood which charity realizes only in the Church and through the Church. Those, finally, who *suffer persecution for justice' sake,* that is, for the Faith and for doing good, *possess the kingdom of Heaven,* because in their sufferings they feel they possess the sure title to heavenly happiness, and for them, recompense on earth consists in their firm hope of possessing God.

This happiness which the beatitudes give and the world cannot grasp – because it lives on illusions and in the mire – is only a taste of the eternal happiness, the reward to him who attains heroic virtue. Without doubt, Paradise is perfect happiness, the common recompense of all the beatitudes; but this recompense is presented under a particular and different aspect, in harmony with the special merit gained from each of them. Thus, for those on earth who are *little and poor of spirit* out of love for God, Paradise is the riches of happiness and glory, or is for them *a kingdom*. For those who are *meek*, Paradise is the empire of hearts living on earth: *they shall possess the earth*. For those *who mourn*, Paradise becomes pure consolation without end: *they shall be comforted*. For those *who hunger and thirst for justice*, because they cannot stand abuse of power and dishonesty – hoping in divine justice, Paradise is the perfect satisfaction of their yearning: *they shall be satisfied*. For *the merciful*, Paradise is having the recompense of eternal happiness *with the same mercy*. For *the pure of heart*, Paradise is the very vision of God: *they shall see God*. For *the peacemakers*, Paradise is the glorious name and incomparable privilege of the children of God: *they shall be called children of God*. For those *who suffer persecution for justice' sake*, the reward is Paradise itself which *they conquer* in exchange for their sacrifice.

To THIS HARMONY is added another: the ascending order of eternal recompense. The common recompense of all the Blessed is to *have* Paradise. The second is *to possess it*, which is certainly more than having it, and hence to experience the eternal security of possession. The third is to be *comforted* in the possession of Paradise, or to have the enjoyment of God, which is more than having and possessing it. The fourth is to be *satisfied*, and hence to have the superabundance of consolation in the possession of God. The fifth gives us as measure of consolation, not justice strictly proportioned to merits and to desires, but to *mercy*, ever exuberant. The sixth gives us as consolation *the vision of God*. The seventh brings us close to God as *sons*, giving us by adoption, a strict right to eternal glory as our inheritance. The eighth gives us eternal glory by means of suffering for Jesus Christ as our conquest. Thus St. Thomas concludes: *In such wise the goal of all the virtues, of all the gifts and of all the beatitudes of the Holy Spirit, is to lead man, step by step, to the supreme dignity of son of God and therefore of brother and coheir of Jesus Christ.*

II. Heroism to Which the Beatitudes Elevate by Means of the Gifts of the Holy Spirit from Which They Flow

We have already given a sufficiently clear and complete idea of those supernatural activities which produce the beatitudes in the soul; but now we propose to amplify that presentation, because the beatitudes are the highest peak of perfection to which we are called, both as Christians, and – still more – as priests, if we have been chosen to be such, or as persons consecrated to God.

We call this practice of high virtue *Beatitudes*, in view of the joyful effect, temporal and eternal, which they produce in the soul, and because Jesus Christ taught this path of holiness by repeating the word *blessed*, or happy, to introduce each canon of this method; but these rules constitute a veritable treatise of perfection, and define the heroism at which the virtues, the grace, and gifts of the Holy Spirit must arrive to make us saints and then, blessed in Paradise.

Asceticism, mysticism and the treatises on higher perfection, when one ponders them, are all about this sublime science of the *gifts*, of the *fruits*, and of the *beatitudes* of the Holy Spirit. He who studies in depth and meditates on this science, gradually raises himself from the practice of common virtues to that of the higher virtues and of heroism, until he attains perfect union with God on earth, and immortal glory in Paradise.

The exercise of the *virtues* entails a daily combat, which gives us the satisfaction of victory. The *gifts* give us a great docility of will, which makes possible the action of the Holy Spirit in us and brings us to the perfection of the virtues, conferring on us greater ease in exercising them more perfectly. The gifts, in fact, perfect the basic virtues of Christian life: *faith, hope and charity; prudence, justice, fortitude and temperance*. The *fruits* make us conquer the works of the flesh, balancing the soul, the body, the faculties, the senses, life, and giving us in these exercises of virtue a spiritual taste which not only makes the way of holiness easy, but delightful. The *beatitudes* lift us to the heroism of holiness on earth, give the soul the blessedness of loving union with God, and in Paradise eternal happiness by means of the perfection of union with God and the enjoyment of God.

It is necessary to acknowledge and confess that on the part of Christians, the great ignorance of the action of the Holy Spirit in their souls is the principal cause for which the spirit of the world prevails in them. Virtue is almost totally neglected; holiness is rare – very rare – even in souls consecrated to God, and the decay of the spirit is general and worrisome. Nature has prevailed in every area, and sadly triumphed.

The energies expended to restore Christian spirit are sterile, because these consist mostly in propaganda activity, instead of profound transformation and sanctification. Souls are held to more or less artificial rules of spiritual life, and ignore the sublime rule of the action of the Holy Spirit, the only person who possesses the great secret of supernatural fruitfulness. It is for this reason that we feel the need to further deepen our understanding of the path of the beatitudes, which brings us to the heroism of the virtues and to true perfection and sanctity.

1) Blessed are the poor in spirit, for theirs is the kingdom of heaven. – The world calls blessed, those who abound in earthly goods, and above all wealth and pleasures. Attachment to riches and their unrestrained, disorderly use, materializes life. Pleasures disorder it, because they plunge it into an abyss of sin. The world, in fact, knows only the pleasures of sin which are the accursed works of the flesh: adultery, fornication, impurity, lust, drunkenness, carousing, and like horrors which give the illusion of a richly enjoyable life charged with emotion, a life which the world stupidly defines as *glamorous*.

Jesus Christ calls souls not only to the exercise of the virtues which prevents their falling into the abyss of eternal perdition, but calls them to the heroism of complete detachment from the world and teaches them *poverty of spirit*; He teaches that, with an expression calculated to attract us, calling *blessed* those who practice it. He does not say simply: *Be poor in spirit*, but: *Blessed are the poor in spirit*, that the soul in search of happiness and appropriate satisfaction might be attracted, not by a counsel or a command, but by an invitation to happiness, to the happiness which gives as fruit, that which is eternal: *Blessed are the poor in spirit, for theirs is the kingdom of heaven.*

With this wonderful form of teaching used for all the heroic virtues suggested in the eight beatitudes, Jesus does not force or dominate the human will and freedom, but, in charming it, draws it. If I say to someone: *Be poor in spirit*, this may arouse resistance in him; if I say: *Blessed are the poor in spirit*, and say this with an accent on truth, on sweetness, and love which only Jesus can have, I arouse in him a desire; and if I speak to him of the reward he will have – a reward corresponding with his inmost and highest aspirations – I charm him and conquer him.

Poverty of spirit entails detachment of the heart from earthly goods, a detachment which is an effect of the grace of the Holy Spirit. This detachment can be *internal*, for those who still retain the material possession of their riches; it can be *internal and external* detachment for those who, according to the counsel of the Savior, voluntarily give away all they own for love of Him; it can also be detachment of the heart from aspirations to riches, or simply to prosperity, in those who patiently bear want and other scarcities of life.

Various Fathers of the Church understand by poor in spirit, the humble of heart, and this could very well have been the meaning of the Redeemer, all the more so because in the beatitude immediately following, He speaks of the *meek*. Now, when He wishes us to learn of Him, He speaks of these two virtues jointly: *Learn of me, for I am meek and humble of heart* [Mt 11: 29]. It is also holy poverty of spirit to acknowledge ourselves spiritually poor, namely, in need of divine assistance.

This first beatitude proceeds from the first gift of the Holy Spirit, namely, *Wisdom*, since a property of this gift is to make us understand the vanity of earthly goods in relation to Heaven, thus preventing the heart's attachment to them.

2) BLESSED ARE the meek, for they shall possess the earth. – They are meek who in the afflictions of life and in the injuries done to them, do not allow themselves to be dominated by anger, but with patience and humility, submit to the dispositions of divine Providence and voluntarily pardon those who have offended them, overcoming the strife of sadness with gentleness. The promise which Jesus made to them *to possess the land* regards both time and eternity. In time, the meek *possess the land*, because by their gentleness, they exert a kind of lordship of love and conquer hearts. Good conduct, in fact, and gentleness in dealings, conquer and overcome far more than the sword; the kind man has no enemies, because he confounds them with his calm gentleness, and compels them to empathize with him.

In eternity the meek *will possess the earth* or the happiness prepared by God for his elect, symbolized *in the promised land*, according to what is written in Psalm 36: 29: *The just shall inherit the land, and shall dwell in it forever.* This beatitude – opposed to anger, which is an outburst without discernment – derives from the gift of *Counsel,* giving balance to life, and from that, *knowledge*, which makes us discern things for what they are in the order of God, and our neighbor for what he is in his weaknesses, giving the soul delight and peace.

3) BLESSED ARE they who mourn, for they shall be comforted. – Those who mourn are those who suffer, either from the adversities of life or from physical illness. If they suffer out of love for God and in perfect union with the divine Will, their suffering brings into the soul an ineffable joy, a deep consolation, which can be likened to those bitter tonics which bring bitterness into the mouth, but are delicious because they are aperitifs for the stomach, stimulating the appetite and then making the food exquisitely good-tasting and healthy. Is not the worker consoled in the pains of his labor by the profit that enriches him, and makes his life more comfortable?

He who suffers knows how to merit by reason of the union which he has with the sufferings of Jesus Christ, and is animated to suffer with joy; he knows how to purify himself in pains, and verifies in his torment, the consolation of one who bathes, of one who cures a wound with alcohol that burns, of one who undergoes surgery because he knows it will cure him.

Blessed are tears! If they are the shedding of our delusions, those tears, while they are being shed, are like a veil which on being drawn from the eyes, makes us see life in its sad reality, and makes us also catch a glimpse of the sublime reality of eternal life. If they are tears shed in repentance, they become a laver of purification which, like hydrogen peroxide or mercurial disinfectant, detach the bandage to medicate the wound. If their shedding of tears arises from physical pain, they serve to sound the harmonious tones of sacrifice from the flesh as from taut strings. If they are shed out of love, their mournful cry pierces the heavens and does it violence, that God not resist, but give to the heart what it asks. Did Jesus Himself not say this? [cf. Mt 11:12]. As he wept, the prodigal was embraced by his father and clothed anew: he sorrowed over the disillusionment of his life of luxury [Lk 15:11–32]. The weeping Magdalen was pardoned; and in the tenderness of her love, she wept out of sorrow for her sins [cf Lk 7:36 ff.; 8:2]. The widow of Naim wept over the casket of her only son, and saw him alive once again [Lk 7:11–17]. Jesus, Himself, wept at the tomb of Lazarus, already dead four days, and raised him [Jn 11:1 ff.]; He wept over Jerusalem [Lk 19:41–44], over ungrateful mankind, and redeemed it.

But above all, those who wept here below will be comforted in eternity, because it is written that *God will wipe away every tear from their eyes* [Apoc 7:17], and will shower eternal consolations upon them. The pains suffered during life are, as it were, the secret *to tasting* eternal joys, as hunger is the secret to tasting food; and weariness is the secret to consolation in repose and appreciation for God, and for evaluating material things by means of the intellectual gifts: *Wisdom, Understanding, Counsel and Knowledge* and are fruits of *Fortitude* and of *Godliness* through which one is enabled to suffer; and of *Fear of the Lord,* precisely deriving sighs of repentance and humility in the soul, attracting God to itself.

4) BLESSED ARE they who hunger and thirst for justice, for they shall be satisfied. – A characteristic sign of great souls is the ardent desire for justice, because they love the laws of God, flee disorder, and are on fire with charity. This desire becomes pressing in them, like the need to eat and drink when one is hungry and thirsty, since in the sorrows of injustice and human corruption they feel, as it were, gnawed at, and their heart dried up from the pang. They love the truth and see error and lies in the world; they love order and see disorder; they love good and see evil; they love the right of each and above all the right of God, and see domineering and impiety. They burn with zeal, hungering and thirsting for the glory of God and the salvation of souls; and to them, their every effort seems a failure, because the world continues along its ruinous path, indeed seems ever to worsen. Their hunger and thirst, however, are not in vain because it is not sorrow alone, but the impetus of prayer and action; and God answers their prayer and makes fruitful their activity.

The desire for justice arises within them from love of God and neighbor, and from the fear of God; their hope is proportionate to their hunger and thirst, lest they ever despair of the victory of good; this unshakable hope makes them lively and full of courage in conquering evil opposition. This beatitude, therefore, derives from the gift of Wisdom which perfects charity; from the gift of Fear of the Lord, which is related to hope and perfection; and from the gift of Fortitude.

In time, God responds to love with great works which he stirs up in the Church; and in eternity, he responds with perfect, final justice. He responds to the fear and to the hope of the soul with extraordinary manifestations of his justice: in time at the end of the ages, with the conflagration of the created; and in eternity, with the final sentence of the universal judgment. And he also responds to the natural courage of the soul who, for his love, is afire with zeal, sustaining the soul with supernatural courage. It is thus that the soul who hungers and thirsts for justice *is satisfied* in its love, in its charity for souls, in its zeal, and in its hope in time and in eternity.

Hunger and thirst for justice are also the equivalent of the desire for holiness because, in Scripture, *justice* is also synonymous with sanctity. Now, the soul can have the burning desire to be a saint and to see the earth enriched by saints. When this desire is not a sterile velleity, but ardent and alive like hunger and thirst, and just as imperious as these two natural exigencies, God consoles and satisfies the soul.

The desire for holiness is a beatitude fulfilled, that is, in the attainment of sanctity; and the soul, while on earth, possessing a desire to experience such grace, is sanctified by the Holy Spirit in its lifetime, and is fully satisfied in eternity, because that soul is living in concert with the saints and sees how God responds to the hunger and thirst of those who were its contemporaries. But even before the soul's entrance into Paradise, the Kingdom of God – on the day of the final and universal Judgment, the soul's two ardent desires for justice and holiness are satisfied by the irrevocable sentences of the Divine Judge: *Depart from me, accursed ones, into the everlasting fire; come, blessed of my Father, take possession of the Kingdom* [cf. Mt 25:34, 41].

5) Blessed are the merciful, for they shall find mercy. – The merciful are those who have pity for the miseries of others, both spiritual and corporal, and seek to alleviate them with appropriate works of mercy. The spiritual works of mercy are seven: counsel the doubtful, instruct the ignorant, admonish sinners, console the afflicted, pardon offenses, patiently bear with boring persons, pray to God for the living and the dead. The works of corporal mercy are seven: feed the hungry, give drink to the thirsty, clothe the naked, give shelter to pilgrims, care for the sick, visit the imprisoned, bury the dead. As it stands written that we shall be judged by the same measure by which we have measured others [cf. Lk 6: 38], so it is logical that the Lord will respond with his mercy to those who have been merciful.

We who are so full of miseries and needs must have great mercy for others, above all in compassion, in consoling, in forgiving, and in assisting. Mercy, by its very nature, is a beatitude, because it opens the soul and the heart to a great satisfaction and peace, and makes them feel the sweetness of God's grace poured forth in them. Further, it is a beatitude in view of the reward it merits from God in time and in eternity: in time with spiritual and temporal blessings with which God mercifully responds to our mercy; in eternity with the blessing which will be ours in the last judgment and with the glory of Paradise. It is no accident, and it is supremely important to reflect on this, that the Lord should tell us how he will examine us and how he will judge us solely on the basis of our charity and our works of mercy. Imagine all the many responsibilities of our life being judged – and they are countless! But he limits himself to mentioning only mercy, because on that tremendous day, we will all have great need of the mercy of God, and only under the shadow of those immense wings can we be saved.

The beatitude of mercy derives from the gift of Godliness; rather it is the gift of Godliness in action, which when referred to one's neighbor, dissolves and appears as the radiation of works of Christian mercy.

6) Blessed are the pure of heart, for they shall see God. – By pure of heart, one must understand not only those who are not contaminated by sin, but in a special way *the chaste, the continent, and the virgins.* They *shall see God* even on earth, namely they will know him in the clearest of light, understand him with the deepest of understanding, love him with the most burning love, and hence, they *will see* him with their inner eye, because they place no obstacle to the communication of their love to him, and to the thrust of their love toward him.

Thereby, a flood of love invades the soul like the purest ray of charity flowing forth from God. When the soul is pure, it receives this ray without foggy obstruction of any kind; when the soul is not pure, this ray is extinguished in the soul, and the outpouring of grace does not reach it. The soul then resembles the dense atmosphere of a dark cloud; the fog condenses into water, the water falls upon the earth as rain, then mixes with the earth to form mud. How can the divine flood mingle with the muddy earth; how can the divine ray shine in a swamp?

The impure soul, moreover, is totally concentrated on one entirely materialistic viewpoint, and sees only what bears on the miserable satisfaction of the senses. The pure soul, instead, is not so narrow-minded; fleeing from what might contaminate it, it sees God by means of the wonders he has created, marveling at their harmony in him: contemplating him in the beauty of flowers; admiring him in the immensity of the starry heavens; pondering him in the power of the roaring seas; hearing him in the voice of prayer. And everything reminds the soul of God so convincingly that it can be said *to see him.* This contemplative vision, then, is the prelude to the beatific vision, which is more brilliant for such a soul, than for those who were defiled on earth. The latter have a lower degree of glory and retain, so to speak, a certain myopia even in Paradise which, if not opposed to their happiness, always entails a lesser degree of intensity in the beatific vision.

Purity also brings with it a special entitlement to glory in Heaven; and for this reason, it is said that the virgins follow the Lamb wheresoever He goes and sing a canticle no others can sing [cf. Apoc 14:3].

The beatitude of purity which, more than any other, brings us to the knowledge and to the enjoyment of God proceeds from the gift of *Fortitude*, insofar as it is victory over the flesh; and from the gift of *Understanding*, insofar as it is a more vast and more profound knowledge of God and of the supernatural virtues.

With what love must we guard cleanliness of heart, fountain of inestimable good and of inestimable joy! With what care must we wear before God our virginal mantle, when we have the good fortune of never having sullied it, and of having been called to a holy vocation or to the priesthood, or to the virginal or religious state!

7) Blessed are the peacemakers, for they shall be called children of God. – Peacemakers of whom we speak are not, strictly speaking, the meek. These latter are only those who do not respond to evil with evil, whereas peacemakers respond to evil with good; they bring accord where there is discord, tranquillity where there is agitation, peace where there is war. This peace which they pour forth all about them, derives from a sage assessment and balanced evaluation of the circumstances of human life that comes to them from the gift of Counsel, which can indeed be described in them as Counsel in action.

By reason of this gift, they are balanced in judgment, merciful in condemning, sweet and tactful in reproving, maternal in chastising, and always find every appropriate means for promoting and keeping peace. They subdue and enlighten those who explode with rage; and just as oil spread on the waters calms the tempest, so with their persuasive and prudent words, they reduce and calm the storms of souls, as it were, with the oil of sweetness. Hence, *they are called children of God*, because they gather their brethren into the unity of peace, keeping the Lord's family undivided for him; they are called children of God because they mirror and imitate his mercy. And God loves them with a special love, regarding them as his favorite children in the family of the Catholic Church.

Peacemakers are those who guard his peace in their hearts, fleeing the agitations of the spirit, living in confidence and abandonment to God *as his children* who struggle during life, but trust in him; who do not uselessly vent their feelings with murmuring against their neighbor; who are not devious in their dealings, but in all find motives of interior calm! God hates rumor-mongers who sow discord; and he does not come down to stormy souls who, like the waves of the sea, spread their disturbance to others as well, stirring up more tempests; hence we should guard, within and about ourselves, the tranquil peace of the children of God, because it is the secret of blessedness during the exile of earthly life, which anticipates the ineffable peace of eternity.

8) BLESSED ARE they who suffer persecution for justice' sake, for theirs is the kingdom of Heaven. – This is the beatitude related to the struggle of God's children in the combat waged against them by the world and the devil. It is the beatitude of heroism which does not yield to evil, immolates itself for the truth, and accepts disdain as sign of God's love. For in persecution, one experiences oneself as a favorite of God and as one closest to him. It is the beatitude of martyrdom which, in the midst of curses and torments, preserves the treasures of faith, hope, charity, and purity, and rises victorious in suffering and in death itself. It is the joy of not becoming disheartened in humiliation, of holding high the ravaged standards of glorious combat on the invincible rock of justice, truth, and holiness [cf. Mt 7:24–27]. Hence, in the context of this specific beatitude, Jesus Christ is resolute, applying to it words of greater urgency. For this beatitude is the battle cry which He consigns to souls who must spread His kingdom, and to the Church which must conserve His throne intact amidst the tide of events, human malice, and the tempests unleashed against them by the devil.

Blessed are you, He exclaims, *when men reproach you and persecute you, and speaking falsely, say all manner of evil against you for my sake. Rejoice and exult because your reward is great in heaven, because thus did they persecute the prophets who were before you.* There is a savor of interior sweetness present in such souls, amidst the curses that are heaped upon them, because they lean on God alone and cast themselves solely on him, knowing that they are afflicted on account of the truth. In this way, there is a profound detachment from living a lie – which the world is – while one is calumniated for God's sake; because then, one's conscience feels judged by him alone, who is truth, wisdom, and love. Herein also rests the certainty of eternal recompense, attained at the cost of suffering. This assurance makes the soul rejoice and exult, as do the martyrs when, in their anguish and torments, they see the barrier collapse, which had previously separated them from total union with God. There is the exultation of belonging to that host of heroes; and after death, the world finally renders a true assessment of their lives, although it had inflicted ridicule and persecution upon them during their lifetime [cf. Wisdom 2:10–24; 5:1–15]. For those persecuted out of love for Him, Jesus plans their glorification even on earth and the glory of paradise awaiting them, when they are finally united in the splendor of that army of warriors of truth, goodness, and love, of which the world is unworthy.

As is evident, this beatitude derives from the gift of *Fortitude,* but is supported and animated by all seven gifts. For the soul does not reach the heroism of love for God to the point of self-sacrifice without being illumined by the gifts of Wisdom, of Understanding, of Counsel, and of Knowledge. These gifts make the soul know and appreciate him above all things. Nor can the soul reach such heroism without having for God and neighbor, a tender love and profound respect, which the soul can enjoy superabundantly only via the gifts of Godliness and Fear of the Lord.

IN VIRTUE OF the promise of Jesus Christ, then, all the virtues produce the fruit of eternal life. For this reason, the heroic acts of the virtues performed on these sublime heights of the human spirit, are called beatitudes. Eternal happiness, however, which Jesus promises, is not given to all equally and under the same form: for the poor of spirit, it is a kingdom; for the meek, a land of infinite value; for those who mourn, a consolation; for those who hunger and thirst for justice, a banquet; for the clean of heart, a special vision of God; for the peacemakers, a divine filiation which entails, as well, a right to a divine inheritance; for the persecuted, victory, joy, conquest, and a kingdom of glory.

The tree of eternal happiness [cf. Ps 1: 3], perfumed and budding forth flowers even during temporal life, has its roots in poverty of spirit, and hence not in the muddy soil of the world, but in the Kingdom of God. It grows in gentle serenity when watered by contradictions. For it is the young shoot which, amidst the fury of the wind, does not snap. During the night of pilgrimage, it prospers on the flood of tears watering it, and is nourished and fertilized by the sap of justice, and by trials which bring with them its proper holiness. It flourishes on mercy; through purity, it is rendered fruitful by the eternal Sun; bears its fruit in the warm love of God's peace; and when cut down by persecutions, is transplanted to the halls of the Kingdom of God. Had the world understood these wonderful ways of joy, it would not have smothered itself in stupid and criminal orgies, causing it bitterness even in the present life, as if incinerated in burning flames and buried in volcanic ash – leading to eternal perdition.

✠

The Charisms of the Holy Spirit

CR

I. Charisms of the Holy Spirit: Their Names – Concepts – The Listing of St. Paul – Modern Prejudices Against the Charisms

The gifts of the Holy Spirit are directed principally to the sanctification of the soul which receives them, and hence, are called by theologians, *graces which make one pleasing to God*: *gratiae gratum facientes*. We say they are ordered *principally* to the soul who receives them, because in sanctifying it, elevating it, and making it supernaturally fruitful to the point of heroism in the practice of the virtues, they are indirectly beneficial to others as well. In fact, there exists nothing else on earth so beneficial to a truly Christian soul, and even more, to a holy soul.

There are, however, other gifts of the Holy Spirit which are principally and directly oriented to the welfare and sanctification of others, without in themselves, necessarily adding any benefit to the privileged soul enriched by them, and, *in theory*, not requiring holiness in the person receiving them. We say that these gifts are directly oriented to others and, that in theory, they do not require holiness in the one enriched by them, although in reality, they do indirectly also benefit the one receiving them. In general, they are given to complement the activities of a holy life as a sign and a splendor of such a life. Especially since the spread of the Church throughout the world, it is very rare, not to say impossible, to find one endowed with such extraordinary gifts who is not a saint. And when perchance, such a person be found who is not a saint, one should be on guard against diabolical deception to discern in that case what is from God, and what comes from Satan, from occult powers, or morbid excitation.

To distinguish the *gratuitous* gifts, or *gratis data*, of the Holy Spirit from those which render the soul pleasing to God, a Greek word is employed, *charisms*, which means *gifts*, but which has the advantage of avoiding confusion between these two categories of gifts. The *charisms*, therefore, may be defined thus: *Gratuitous gifts, extraordinary and passing, bestowed by the Spirit to the advantage of other souls, or to the edification of the Church*. St. Paul, in his first Letter to the Corinthians [14: 1 ff.] lists nine: *language of revelation (or wisdom), language of knowledge, gift of faith, gift of healing, gift of miracles, gift of prophecy, discernment of spirits, gift of tongues, gift of interpretation*. To these nine, he adds six others in the Letter to the Romans [12: 6–8] after mentioning *prophecy*, included in the foregoing list: *ministry, teaching, exhorting, giving to others what is theirs, presiding, exercising works of mercy*. But even with these, the list cannot be said to be exhaustive, but only an extensive exemplification.

According to St. Paul, followed by St. Thomas Aquinas, these charisms are inferior to charity, to sanctifying grace, and to the sevenfold gifts of the Holy Spirit. Whereas in fact, without the mediation of other entities – the gifts, grace, and charity effect union of the soul with the Holy Spirit – the charisms only prepare souls for these gifts via a manifestation of an action of the Holy Spirit. Hence, St. Paul exhorts the Corinthians not to become proud or boast of these gifts, but rather to compete in finding others much better, namely, those that sanctify the recipients of these gifts.

In any case, in speaking of the superiority of the gifts over the charisms, it is not our intention to establish greater or lesser value within the same category, as if the charisms had less value or less efficacy than the gifts; in fact, for the scope for which they were or are given, they are supremely important in the development and spiritual progress of the

Church, performing a demonstrative and apologetic role of the first order. This is why, in the earliest days, of the Church, we observe a luxuriant flourishing of the most stupendous charisms. Such a continuous and generous employment of the sensational, external, visible, and overwhelming supernatural events was required in those times, for the establishment of the Church among pagans and infidels.

In the following ages these diminish, because the Church had already sunk deep roots, but they did not disappear nor are they disappearing. A learned modern author[12] writes thus:

Deposited in the bosom of the Church on the day of Pentecost they will remain as its adornment until the last day. The lives of recently canonized Saints of the Church offer, in fact, such a richness of charisms, that often the pretentious Christian mentality of our days finds itself overwhelmed and troubled. Unfortunately almost all of us have contracted from that dominant rationalism of the 19th century a tragic repugnance for sensational and marvelous events, and the effort expended by so many modern biographers of saints to reduce to the bare minimum the charismatic and miraculous aspects of those whose lives they are recounting is pitiful. They show not the slightest realization that this open and triumphant action of the divine Spirit in the saints is the most splendid golden foundation for depicting them... Without that divine Spirit one ends by describing the heroes of Heaven in terms identical with those of earth.

We would also add that the sterility in charisms and supernatural manifestations in modern circles is due precisely to this dull modern spirit, sadly reinforced by an insidious and disguised modernist propaganda, conducted with the tools of criticism, science and even boasting a morally responsible seriousness. Moreover, the diabolical multiplicity of diviners, palm readers, spiritualists, etc., has confused many minds, and leading the naïve and simple-minded to identify such

---

12 D. Fausto Mezza in his golden book: *Lo Spirito Santo vita dell'anima* [The Holy Spirit, Life of the Soul].

insidious, diabolical rubbish with the charisms of the Holy
Spirit has, in their eyes, discredited the divine gifts, disoriented
their souls, and caused the naïve and simple-minded to reject
and despise these charisms.

The confusion has also been increased by certain erroneous
medical theories, which consider the evident charisms of the
Holy Spirit on a par with morbid phenomena characteristic of
psychic and nervous disorders. To their shame and misfortune,
even famous physicians, materialists, rationalists and infidels,
have claimed to take charge of mystics on the basis of
preconceived ideas. In so doing, they have cut the sad figure
of the street-sweeper who – only because he has a brush with
which to sweep – takes up painting and sketches the most
repulsive designs with that brush, happily presuming they
are on a level with the Transfiguration by Raphael or the Last
Judgment by Michelangelo.

The comparison may seem a bit harsh, but if these people
can put the divine charisms on a level with pathological
disorders – and on the other hand, if one can appreciate the
enormous difference separating the two sets of phenomena
– one must admit that the comparison still remains much too
bland. The deplorable ignorance of these physicians in matters
divine is alarming; their obvious inexperience in manifestations
of grace is lamentable. And a book on mysticism in their hands
is more obscure and confounding to them than a libretto
of superb music in the hands of a skilled metal worker, to
say the least – or more precisely, in the hands of a fashion
designer who, upon seeing black dots on a white background,
cannot even imagine that the dots on a masterful composition
by Beethoven are expressions of sublime, sweet, and ecstatic
melodies.

II. Charisms of the Holy Spirit in Particular

Before all else, the charisms of *Revelation (Wisdom)* and
of *Knowledge*, with which St. Paul begins his listing, are not

the same as the gifts of the Holy Spirit which we have already considered; and for this reason, the Apostle does not simply say *Wisdom and Knowledge*, but he says: *the language of Wisdom, the language of Knowledge*. These make possible the translation into appropriate language of the most sublime theological concepts and the most convincing philosophical arguments for proving revealed truths. More exactly the *language of Wisdom* helps to deduce from the truths of Faith, considered as principles, conclusions enriching our knowledge of dogmas. The *language of Knowledge* makes it possible to take advantage of human sciences to explain the truths of Faith.

With these two charisms, even an unlearned soul can speak with exact precision of language and with great insight on truths of the Faith, as can be read in the lives of so many humble laymen and simple women. They became great souls because of a divine charism and were even consulted by famous individuals and illustrious scientists because of the luminous clarity of their thoughts. Thus do we read in the lives of St. Catherine of Siena; St. Paschal Baylon, a simple Franciscan brother; St. Gerard Majella, a humble Redemptorist lay brother, and numerous others.

THE CHARISM OF faith, which follows, should not be confused with the virtue of faith nor with the fruit of the Holy Spirit which bears the same name. A soul might have the virtue and the gift of faith without possessing the charism. The charism of faith lends a special certainty to revealed truths, and tends to the production of prodigies and extraordinary things in order to demonstrate the truths of revelation and of the promises of Jesus Christ.

Very similar to this charism are those of *healing* and of *miracles*, since these extraordinary manifestations of the power of God always tend to confirm the Faith. The charism of *healings* is restricted solely to cases of illness to be cured; that of the *working of miracles* extends to other prodigies, including the resurrection of the dead. The Lord raises up souls who are, as it were, supernatural physicians: by consoling and healing the infirm they act in charity and confirm the grandeur of the faith. In addition, he raises up thaumaturgists who work wonders in the most unusual circumstances, and confirm those whose faith is unstable. The lives of the saints, both men and women, are replete with these manifestations of divine power.

THE CHARISM OF *prophecy* consists in the power that the Holy Spirit gives to certain souls to foresee the future, and also to see things far off that cannot be known by natural means, whether mechanical or psychic. The prophet sees future things in a clear light of evidence, as though they were present; and he sees them by means of internal or external symbols that manifest to him the future in synthetic form, of which he himself gives the explanation or perceives the meaning.

The solemn prophecies through which God announced the Incarnation of his Son are evidently closed. The great prophets – who spoke to mankind and to former ages about the development of history and the general events regarding the world and the Church – have no further reason to be. There are, however, souls in the Church endowed with prophetic spirit who privately proclaim, as it were, and within limited range, the imminent chastisements that are to strike mankind or matters regarding specific persons. These prophets should not be confused with charlatans or diviners who, via occult forces, whether natural or diabolical, can know future, non-contingent events which are certain – and whose occurrence may depend on natural processes already developing, yet not evident, i.e., an earthquake, a cyclone, the death of a dear one, etc.

Regrettably, professional diviners who charge exorbitant fees for their soothsaying, have tremendously increased in number, as has their wealth, because most people have at least a mild curiosity to know the future. God does not speak through these frauds; and it is forbidden to consult with them since one always runs the risk of being duped, either by their stratagem or by Satan.

Part of the gift of prophecy is to teach or to preach, in the name of God, with inspired words that move and penetrate souls. One who has this gift of the Holy Spirit, does not announce new, future events, but transports the soul into a supernatural realm and fills it with the living light of the truths he proclaims. We must admit that modern-day preaching is impoverished of this gift, as are so many writers on sacred subjects, who drift about in the clouds and fail to interest or move souls to compunction; or they simply limit themselves to a purely natural sphere that cannot produce supernatural fruits. Worse still, if leaving aside the spirit of God, they speak under the influence of the impious, as those who unfortunately rely on the works of rationalists and Protestants in the fields of biblical exegesis, history, and science. The obvious absence of the Holy Spirit in so many Catholic writers and preachers is one of the most deleterious causes of the downfall of peoples and souls.

THE CHARISM OF *discernment of spirits* is the infused gift of reading the secrets of hearts, and of discerning the good spirit from the evil one. The absence of this gift impoverishes the confessional ministry and that of spiritual direction. When a confessor or a director does not succeed in clearly reading the very depth of souls, he is precisely in need of this gift to understand them, to familiarize himself with their particular circumstances, and to guide them. His need for this charism must not only move him to implore it of God, but to lead a life of holiness, totally removed from the maxims and prudence of the world.

It is deplorably shallow to believe that the confessor is simply a listener to the outpourings of a conscience, who limits himself to granting absolution. In so delicate a ministry, it is still more deplorable if he allows himself to be ruled by fixations and personal opinions that might induce souls to a dangerous laxity or an oppressive rigor – both contrary to the teachings of the Church – or a tendency toward false piety which is empty of true virtue and true love of God. When choosing a confessor or director, souls need to pray a great deal; and having made their choice, they must daily invoke the Holy Spirit to give him the discernment of their spirit and of their conscience.

THE CHARISM OF *the gift of tongues,* which was given to the Apostles on the day of Pentecost is, for us, the most obscure and the most discussed, both by exegetes and theologians. In view of the conflicting opinions on this charism, one might say that its discussion oftentimes leads … to the confusion of tongues. This confusion arises from believing that *speaking in various languages* – of which mention is made in the Acts of the Apostles after the descent of the Holy Spirit – is only a single grace.

We will cite the entire text of Acts 2:1 ff., because one can thus clearly see that the prodigy consisted in two manifestations:

1) The Apostles, full of love and all aflame with the Holy Spirit, emerged from the Cenacle praising God in various languages, *even as the Holy Spirit prompted them to speak* [v. 4]; they represented all of mankind, reborn and redeemed, and offered praises of thanks to God in the tongues of the various peoples on earth. It was fitting and logical that the Apostles, in the name and in the languages of all peoples, would perform as first action of their universal ministry, that of rendering praise and thanks to God for the ineffable blessing of the Redemption which had been disavowed by the Hebrews and Romans.

The Apostles did not praise God as one voice, but each one thanked God in one language and another in a different tongue, *even as the Holy Spirit prompted them to speak.* It is indeed legitimate to suppose that each Apostle praised and thanked God in the language of the peoples he would evangelize and, that in their name, he exalted and thanked God for the Redemption as first step to receiving the grace of evangelization afterwards. The prodigy, then, in a first moment, regarded only the Apostles, and it is that which is commonly meant by the Greek term *glossalalia,* namely, *praise of God in another language.* For the Apostles, those languages were naturally unknown, and hence it is said that *they began to speak in foreign (or new) tongues* [v. 4]. This does not mean that they praised God in new languages, hitherto unheard in the world, as some suppose.

2) After having praised God, the Apostles spoke to the people to begin their evangelization; this is perfectly evident from the text and context. The Apostles, in the first moment of the prodigy, did not speak in the square; St. Peter did that immediately afterwards to refute those who claimed they were drunk. The Sacred Text identifies that people of many nations had gathered in that place for the feast of Pentecost and all heard the Apostles speaking the native tongue of each one. They were amazed at this because they not only knew that the Apostles were Hebrews, but that they spoke Aramaic, the language commonly spoken by the Hebrews of that time. It is not improbable that the Hebrews themselves, present in the crowd, made known the miraculous character of the event to the foreigners from other nations who claimed to have understood them. The Apostles praised God in the languages of various peoples, and that miracle occurred in them; afterwards they spoke to the people in one language, but making themselves understood by all, and the second miracle occurred in the people.

Here is the text of Acts 2: 4–11, which leaves no room for equivocations:

*And they were all filled with the Holy Spirit and they
began to speak in foreign tongues,* even as the Holy Spirit
prompted them to speak.

Now there were staying at Jerusalem devout Jews
from every nation under heaven. And when this sound
was heard, the multitude gathered and was bewildered
in mind, because *each heard them speaking in his own
language.* But they were all amazed and marveled, saying:
Behold, are not these who are speaking Galileans? And how
have we heard each his own language in which he was born?
Parthians and Medes and Elamites, and inhabitants of
Mesopotamia, Judea, and Cappadocia, Pontus and Asia,
Phrygia and Pamphylia, Egypt and the parts of Libya
about Cyrene, and visitors from Rome, Jews also and
proselytes, Cretans and Arabians, *we have heard them
speaking in our own languages* of the wonderful works of
God.

It is evident: first *they spoke in various languages* praising
God. Afterwards the pilgrims from various nations of nearly
the entire world then known, each in his own language, heard
the Apostles, speaking only one language, making themselves
understood by all as they spoke *of those great things* wrought by
God in the Redemption, *loquentes magnalia Dei.*

This is the most obvious explanation of the text and of the
context of Acts, and the objections which have been made to
it do not seem to enjoy consistency.

For greater clarity, we briefly examine here a few examples,
because the question is strongly debated and much controverted.
St. Paul, it is objected, describing the miraculous phenomenon
of the glossolalia, says that *he who speaks in tongues, speaks not
to men, but to God.* – St. Paul, we reply, speaks here of one
particular manifestation of the gift of tongues, but does not
exclude other types. – It is objected that St. Peter *made use of
St. Mark as his interpreter.* – And what follows from this? God
does not act superfluously, and to have the gift of tongues does

not mean to have these to use at every moment of the day, nor does it mean that when a natural means is available for some task, that one should presume on a supernatural means.

The gifts and charisms of the Holy Spirit are not like mechanical and physical phenomena, which are realized and always reproduced in the same fashion. Identical in substance, the gifts and charisms are manifested and applied in accord with the souls who have received them, and can have the most variegated nuances from soul to soul. Are not human faces similar? They have eyes, nose, mouth, etc., all of them, yet how many are the endless variations in physiognomy! So, too, is grace; so, too, are the gifts of the Holy Spirit at work in souls.

It is certain that the gift of tongues in the sense of being able to make oneself understood speaking one's own language by one or more peoples of a different language, has been verified many times in the saints, and should have been realized even more among the Apostles. The Holy Spirit descended on the Apostles to unite all mankind in a single family, the Church, which on the day of Pentecost was, as it were, officially constituted and proclaimed in the world.

To confound human pride in the erection of the tower of Babel, God descended and set language into confusion. To unite mankind in the building of the Kingdom of God, the Holy Spirit descended and – in the confused and confusing babel of so many languages of various nations gathered in Jerusalem – wrought two miracles leading to a wonderful union: the praise of God in all the languages spoken by the pilgrims of the nations, and the understanding by all in a single language, to the point of amazement. We should preferably say, that rather than communicate by word, the Apostles communicated with ideas, concepts, and with the light of the truths they proclaimed.

We experience something naturally, which in a rudimentary and remote way has a kind of analogy with this prodigy, when

we communicate by a smile, by signs, or by facial expressions
with persons of other nations and linguistic groupings. There
are no people who do not understand the meaning of a finger
pointing to indicate an object, who do not grasp an expression
of sorrow or of joy, or who do not comprehend a gesture of the
need to drink, to eat, etc. The Church employs these gestures
in wonderful ways in its Liturgy, where she praises God in
every language and makes herself understood by peoples of all
languages. It is thus that she unites the peoples in her bosom,
and communicates and keeps the flame of faith and of piety
burning.

An aspect of the gift of tongues which the Holy Spirit bestows
on missionaries is their ease in mastering and understanding
the language of the peoples they evangelize, and the facility in
making themselves understood. The prodigy of Pentecost has
happened many times in missionary saints; but even when this
does not happen straightaway, it is certainly by the grace and
gift of the Holy Spirit that missionaries communicate with
ease, even with peoples whose language is particularly difficult
to learn.

THE CHARISM OF *interpretation* is the supernatural power to
interpret discourses of someone who has the gift of tongues.
In the earliest ages when the Holy Spirit inflamed a soul in
love, making it praise God in various languages, he also raised
up those who explained the meaning of these bursts of love,
to the common edification of all. In fact, it could also happen
– and often did – that someone, bursting forth in such acts of
love, did not grasp the impact of the meaning of the various
languages he spoke. These outbursts of love which seem so
strange to us today were, at root, an act of reparation for
peoples not yet believing in God, nor yet praising him; and
this form of prayer was made in their name, to merit these
graces for them, as people commonly said of old.

The charism of interpretation does not regard tongues alone, but also – and mainly today – the interpretation of Sacred Scripture, which is the Word of God given to us. With this gift, the Fathers of the Church were enriched in singular fashion; and for this reason it seems rash, to say the least, for us to reject the sense of the Divine Word which they have ascribed to it, by substituting our own interpretation, based either on natural principles or, worse, on rationalistic hypotheses. If the Holy Spirit has given us such luminaries to guide us in the understanding of divine language, and if the Church expounds them in so many ways, who would dare replace them as though worn out tools, considered antiquated? Rather, they are the golden candelabra, as it were, ever burning brightly in the Temple [cf. Apoc 11:4], and the sacred fire ever blazing. Their light and their warmth of love impede us from leaping into the darkness and cold of an erring modernity.

THE CHARISM OF *ministry* is the supernatural disposition to exercise fittingly the various ecclesial ministries with piety, graciousness, and refinement, to the life and edification of souls. One may carry a candlestick in a liturgical service so as to edify those in attendance; or one may carry it with indifference and negligence, as if it were a burdensome task. An acolyte who senses the nobility of his office and performs it supernaturally, is no longer a mere cleric in course of advancement, but an angel resplendent in the Church of God.

THE CHARISM OF *teaching* regards instructors in the Faith, and also civil teachers who realize their dignity as educators. It bestows on them dispositions for performing this office efficaciously. The value and persuasiveness of a teacher are not merely the fruit of study or of natural qualities, but are the fruit of a special grace. Were we convinced that all is the grace of God and that, in reality, we are poorly suited for the actions we perform, we would feel the need and the duty to have recourse to God, to his Divine Spirit, to be guided and vivified in all the actions of our life; we then would not have to confront the deplorable spectacle of teachers whose faith is lifeless, and teachers of science whose instructions corrupt youth.

THE CHARISM OF exhortation disposes one to know how to correct with particular grace and effectiveness, and is more than ever necessary to parents, educators, superiors and all who enjoy any responsibility for the formation of souls. The enormous difficulty encountered in educating today, and the almost complete sterility of admonitions, are the direct result of the absence of this particular charism.

THE CHARISM OF giving to others what is their due, as that *of performing works of mercy,* renders the soul detached from its own things and generous in charity, and enables it to give alms, to care for the needy and the suffering. In the early Church these were gifts bestowed on deacons, deaconesses,[13] and on whoever had the care of the poor and the suffering; today these are gifts to be implored, especially by sisters in active life, nursing brothers, and in general, all who are committed to the works of charity. The lack of these gifts in them produces harshness, impatience, meanness, hardness of heart, and nullifies the apologetic value which works of charity ordinarily have for the Faith and for the Church.

FINALLY *THE CHARISM of presiding* has reference to the gift of organizing, governing and directing. Let us be persuaded that in every activity, we have need of the grace of the Holy Spirit because, of ourselves, we can do nothing; and that which we do or pretend to do with only natural powers, is always sterile of true fruits of good. Even natural dispositions and

---

[13] In the early centuries of the Church, deaconess did not connote a woman who had received the Sacrament of Holy Orders, as deacons did, but was a woman, usually a consecrated virgin or widow, who had charge of works of mercy for the poor.

powers are a gift from God, and the Lord makes use of them when he calls us to a particular mission by means of these natural gifts; and his Providential care disposes that they enjoy conditions favorable to their cultivation; but the various and fecund activities for the good of the Church are always fruit of the special charisms of the Holy Spirit. Hence, instead of glorifying so-called *human ingenuity,* we should glorify God who with his Holy Spirit arouses, develops, and makes fecund all the marvelous activities of his saints and of his Church.

Let us therefore, invoke the Holy Spirit. Filled by him, may we be as plants flourishing in the Church, thus preventing that heartrending spectacle of sterility and inertia we so often manifest, in contrast to the children of darkness who, seduced by the spirit of evil, show themselves shrewder and more active in the shameful works of evil [cf. 16:8–13].

O Holy Spirit, Guest enduring of my soul, remain in me and make me always able to remain in Thee.

✠

Rite of Confirmation Outside of the Mass

Introduction

In Confirmation administered by the Bishop, shepherd of souls, or by his representative, imposition of hands is the act whereby, in the Liturgy, the gifts of God are called down upon the soul of the person receiving the Sacrament. This gesture recalls that by which military captains of old enrolled their soldiers; the anointing recalls that of the shepherd marking his sheep. Athletes of old were anointed with oil so as to be agile while in competition. The Christian is anointed with the oil of chrism so as to be consecrated as an athlete of faith, of which he must never be ashamed, and hence the anointing is on his forehead.

During Confirmation the confirmand is assigned a *godfather* or a *godmother*, to guide and assist him or her in conducting a Christian life. This godparent must therefore be of exemplary life and exercise an office of spiritual paternity or maternity. The godfather or godmother contract a spiritual relationship with the confirmand, but no impediment to marriage arises from this relationship.

To exercise this office *validly*, the godfather or godmother must possess the use of reason and be confirmed themselves; they must not be heretics or schismatics, nor must they have incurred juridical impediments to the office.

The Entrance Rite

[The bishop makes the usual reverence to the altar with the ministers and greets the people:]

Peace be with you. *R.* And also with you.

Let us pray: God of power and mercy, send your Holy Spirit to live in our hearts and make us temples of his glory. We ask this through our Lord Jesus Christ, your Son, who lives and reigns with you and the Holy Spirit, one God, for ever and ever. Amen.

Celebration of the Word of God

Reading or readings are to be chosen from the following passages:

Old Testament: Is 11: 1–4a; Is 42: 1–3; Is 61: 1–3a. 6a. 8b–9; Ez 36: 24–28; Joel 2: 23a. 26–30a.

New Testament: Acts: 1: 3–8; Acts 2: 1–6. 22b–23. 32–33; Acts 8: 1. 4. 14–17; Acts 10: 1. 33–34a. 37–44; Acts 19: 1b–6; Rom 5: 1–2. 5–8; Rom 8: 14–17; Rom 8: 26–27; I Cor 12: 4–13; Gal 5: 16–17. 22–23a. 24–25; Eph 1: 3a. 4a. 13–19a; Eph 4: 1–6.

Responsorial Psalm (Vulgate numbering): 21: 23–24. 26–27. 28. 31–32 [R.: v. 23; or Jn 15: 26–27]; 22: 1–3a. 3b–4. 5–6 [R.: verse 1]; 95: 1–2a. 2b–3. 9–10a. 11–12 [R.: verse 1]; 103: 1ab and 24. 27–28. 30–31. 33–34 [R.: verse 30]; 116: 1. 2 [R.: Acts 1: 8]; 144: 2–3. 4–5. 8–9. 10–11. 15–16. 21 [R.: verse 1b].

Alleluia verse: Jn 14: 16; Jn 15: 26b. 27a; Jn 16: 13a; 14: 26b; Apoc 1: 5a. 6.

Gospel: Mt 5: 1–12a; Mt 16: 24–27; Mt 25: 14–30; Mk 1: 9–11; Lk 4: 16 22a; Lk 8: 4 10a. 11b–15, Lk 10: 21–24; Jn 7: 37b–39; Jn 14: 15–17; Jn 14: 23–26; Jn 15: 18–21. 26–27; Jn 16: 5b–7. 12–13a.

Where more than one reading is chosen, the order of readings is: Old Testament, New Testament, and Gospel.

Homily or Allocution

[A brief homily is given by the Bishop in which he should explain the readings and so lead the candidates, their sponsors and parents, and the whole assembly to a deeper understanding of the mystery of Confirmation. These or similar words may be used:]

On the day of Pentecost the Apostles received the Holy Spirit as the Lord had promised. They also received the power of giving the Holy Spirit to others and so completing the work of Baptism. This we read in the Acts of the Apostles. When Saint Paul placed his hands on those who had been baptized, the Holy Spirit came upon them, and they began to speak in other languages and in prophetic words.

Bishops are successors of the apostles and have this power of giving the Holy Spirit to the baptized, either personally or through the priests they appoint.

In our day, the coming of the Holy Spirit in Confirmation is no longer marked by the gift of tongues, but we know his coming by faith. He fills our hearts with the love of God, brings us together in one faith but in different vocations, and works within us to make the Church one and holy.

The gift of the Holy Spirit which you are to receive will be a spiritual sign and seal to make you more like Christ and more perfect members of His Church. At His baptism by John, Christ himself was anointed by the Spirit and sent out on His public ministry to set the world on fire.

You have already been baptized into Christ and now you will receive the power of His Spirit and the Sign of the Cross on your forehead. You must be witnesses before all the world of His suffering, death, and resurrection; your way of life should at all times reflect the goodness of Christ. Christ gives varied gifts to His Church, and the Spirit distributes them among the members of Christ's body to build up the holy people of God in unity and love.

Be active members of the Church, alive in Jesus Christ. Under the guidance of the Holy Spirit give your lives completely in the service of all, as did Christ, who came not to be served but to serve.

So now, before you receive the Spirit, I ask you to renew the profession of faith you made in baptism or your parents and godparents made in union with the whole Church.

Liturgy of the Sacrament

Renewal of Baptismal Promises

[After the homily the candidates stand and the bishop questions them. To each question the candidates respond together: I do.]

Do you reject Satan and all his works and all his empty promises? I do.

Do you believe in God the Father Almighty, Creator of heaven and earth? I do.

Do you believe in Jesus Christ, his only Son, our Lord, who was born of the Virgin Mary, was crucified, died and was buried, rose from the dead, and is now seated at the right hand of the Father? I do.

Do you believe in the Holy Spirit, the Lord, the giver of life, who came upon the Apostles at Pentecost and today is given to you sacramentally in Confirmation? I do.

Do you believe in the holy Catholic Church, the communion of saints, the forgiveness of sins, the resurrection of the body, and life everlasting? I do.

[The bishop confirms their profession of Faith by proclaiming the Faith of the Church:]

This is our Faith. This is the Faith of the Church. We are proud to profess it in Christ Jesus our Lord.

Imposition of Hands

[The bishop faces the people and with hands joined, sings or says:]

My dear friends: in baptism God our Father gave the new birth of eternal life to his chosen sons and daughters. Let us pray to our Father that he will pour out the Holy Spirit to strengthen his sons and daughters with his gifts and anoint them to be more like Christ the Son of God.

[All pray in silence for a short time. Then the bishop and the priests who will minister the sacrament with him lay hands upon all the candidates (by extending their hands over them). The bishop alone sings or says:]

All powerful God, Father of our Lord Jesus Christ, by water and the Holy Spirit you freed your sons and daughters from sin and gave them new life. Send your Holy Spirit upon them to be their helper and guide. Give them the spirit of wisdom and understanding, the spirit of right judgment [counsel] and courage, the spirit of knowledge and reverence [godliness]. Fill them with the spirit of wonder and awe in your presence [fear of the Lord]. We ask this through Christ our Lord. Amen.

Chrismation [anointing with chrism]

[The bishop dips his right thumb in the chrism and makes the Sign of the Cross on the forehead of the one to be confirmed, as he says:]

N., be sealed with the gift of the Holy Spirit. [The newly confirmed responds:] Amen.

[The bishop says:] Peace be with you. [The newly confirmed responds:] And also with you.

Intercessions

My dear friends: let us be one in prayer to God our Father as we are one in the faith, hope, and love his Spirit gives.

Response: Lord, hear our prayer.

For these sons and daughters of God, confirmed by the gift of the Spirit, that they give witness to Christ by lives built on faith and love: let us pray to the Lord. **R.**

For their parents and godparents who led them in faith, that by word and example they may always encourage them to follow the way of Jesus Christ: let us pray to the Lord. **R.**

For the holy Church of God, in union with N. our Pope, N. our Bishop, and all the bishops, that God, who gathers us together by the Holy Spirit, may help us grow in unity of faith and love until his Son returns in glory: let us pray to the Lord. **R.**

For all men, of every race and nation, that they may acknowledge the one God as Father, and in the bond of common brotherhood seek his kingdom, which is peace and joy in the Holy Spirit: let us pray to the Lord. **R.**

God our Father, you sent your Holy Spirit upon the Apostles, and through them and their successors you give the Spirit to your people. May his work begun at Pentecost continue to grow in the hearts of all who believe. We ask this through Christ our Lord. Amen.

Concluding Rite

Lord's Prayer

Dear friends in Christ, let us pray together as the Lord Jesus Christ has taught:

Our Father, etc.

Blessing

God our Father made you his children by water and the Holy Spirit: may he bless you and watch over you with his fatherly love. Amen.

Jesus Christ the Son of God promised that the Spirit of truth would be with His Church forever: may He bless you and give you courage in professing the true Faith. Amen.

The Holy Spirit came down upon the disciples and set their hearts on fire with love: may he bless you, keep you one in faith and love and bring you to the joy of God's kingdom. Amen.

May Almighty God bless you, the Father, and the Son, † and the Holy Spirit. Amen.

[or Prayer over People]

God our Father, complete the work you have begun and keep the gifts of your Spirit active in the hearts of your people. Make them ready to live Christ's Gospel and eager to do His will. May they never be ashamed to proclaim to all the world Christ crucified, living and reigning forever and ever. Amen.

And may the blessing of Almighty God the Father, and the Son, † and the Holy Spirit, come upon you and remain with you forever. Amen.

Appendix Two

Devotion to the Holy Spirit

Devotion to the Holy Spirit

Devotion to the Holy Spirit began with the Church herself, when on the day of Pentecost the Apostles, gathered in the Cenacle about Mary Most Holy in intense prayer of preparation and received this Divine Spirit under the form of tongues of fire. It is a devotion essential to Christian life, and its weakening brings with it a relaxation of this life and the spread of the spirit of the world.

Pope Leo XIII, with the Encyclical *Divinum Illud* (published 9th May, 1897) precisely recommended this devotion – for the calamitous times in which he lived, and for those which his great heart saw taking form in the world – as an efficacious remedy to combat error and to renew Christian life. *Those unhappy times described by St. Paul seemed to have arrived*, exclaimed the great Pope, *in which men would abandon the faith to believe spirits of error and the doctrine of demons, and now more than ever devotion to the Holy Spirit, who is the Spirit of truth, is necessary* [cf. I Tim 4: 1–5]. It cannot be denied that the sad times to which Leo XIII alludes are on-going more than ever today, and that very many souls are confused by false teachers in all fields. We believe it opportune, therefore, to assemble some prayers which the faithful will find helpful when invoking the Holy Spirit.

Hymn to the Holy Spirit

Come, Creator Spirit, come	Veni, Creator Spiritus
From Thy bright, heavenly throne,	Mentes tuorum visita,
Come, take possession of our souls,	Imple superna gratia,
And make them all Thine own.	Quae tu creasti pectora.
Thou who art called the Paraclete,	Qui diceris Paraclitus,
Best gift of God above,	Altissimi donum Dei,
The living spring, the living fire,	Fons vivus, ignis, caritas,
Sweet unction and true love;	Et spiritalis unctio.

Thou who art sevenfold in Thy grace,	Tu septiformis munere,
Finger of God's right hand,	Digitus Paternae dexterae,
His promise, teaching little ones	Tu rite promissum Patris,
To speak and understand:	Sermone ditans guttura.
O guide our minds with Thy blest light,	Accende lumen sensibus,
With love our hearts inflame,	Infunde amorem cordibus;
And with Thy strength which ne'er decays,	Infirma nostril corporis
Confirm our mortal frame.	Virtute firmans perpeti.
Far from us drive our deadly foe,	Hostem repellas longius,
True peace unto us bring;	Pacemque dones protinus:
And through all perils lead us safe	Ductore sic te praevio
Beneath Thy sacred wing.	Vitemus omne noxium.
Through Thee may we the Father know,	Per te sciamus da Patrem,
Through Thee the eternal Son,	Noscamus atque Filium.
And Thee, the Spirit of them both,	Teque utriusque Spiritum
Thrice blessed Three in One.	Credamus omni tempore.
All glory to the Father be,	Deo Patri sit gloria
With His arisen Son,	Et Filio, qui a mortuis
The same to Thee, great Paraclete	Surrexit, ac Paraclito,
While endless ages run. Amen.	In saeculorum saecula. Amen.

Sequence of the Holy Spirit

Come, Holy Spirit, Light divine,	Veni, Sancte Spiritus,
Make the beams celestial shine	Et emitte coelitus
Of thy radiance bright.	Lucis tuae radium.
Come, Thou Father of the lowly,	Veni, Pater pauperum,
Come, Thou Source of all gifts holy;	Veni, Dator munerum,
Come, our hearts' true Light.	Veni, Lumen cordium.

Thou art perfect to console;	Consolator optime,
Guest enduring of the soul;	Dulcis Hospes animae,
Thou, Refreshment sweet.	Dulce refrigerium.
Our Rest upon the toilsome way;	In labore requies,
Our solace when in passion's sway;	In aestu temperies,
Thou, grief's Paraclete.	In fletu solatium.
O most blessed Light, impart	O Lux beatissima,
Thy brightness to the inmost heart	Reple cordis intima
Of those still dear to thee.	Tuorum fidelium.
Without Thy grace to help and guide,	Sine tuo numine,
Man has naught that doth abide,	Nihil est in homine,
Naught from evil free.	Nihil est innoxium.
To wash away each sordid stain,	Lava quod est sordidum,
To heal the wounded, do Thou deign;	Riga quod est aridum,
The parched soul bedew.	Sana quod est saucium.
Do Thou bend the rigid will;	Flecte quod est rigidum,
The frozen heart with fervor fill;	Fove quod est frigidum,
The straying soul renew.	Rege quod est devium.
Thy sacred sevenfold gifts unlock	Da tuis fidelibus
To Thy true and faithful flock	In te confidentibus
Who put their trust in Thee.	Sacrum septenarium.
Grant the prize of virtue's pleading;	Da virtutis meritum,
Grant at death a joyous greeting;	Da salutis exitum,
Grant us bliss eternally. Amen.	Da perenne gaudium. Amen.
(T.P. Alleluia)	

V. Send forth thy Spirit and there will be a new creation.

R. And thou shalt renew the face of the earth.

Let us pray. O God who didst enlighten the faithful by the light of the Holy Spirit: grant that we might be ever wise in the same Spirit and ever rejoice in his consolation. Through Christ our Lord. Amen.

Invocations of the Holy Spirit

(from *Various Prayers* of the Missal)

To obtain the gift of tears

Omnipotent and gentle God who, to slake the thirst of thy people, didst make a fountain of living water gush forth from the rock, draw from our hard hearts tears of compunction, that we might weep over our sins and, by thy mercy, merit to gain their forgiveness.

Kindly pour into our hearts, Lord God, the grace of the Holy Spirit which, with cries and tears, will blot out the stain of our sins and, by thy generosity, obtain for us their long sought pardon. Through Christ our Lord.

To drive away evil thoughts

Omnipotent and kind God, graciously hear our prayers and free our hearts from the temptations of wicked thoughts, that we might merit to become worthy abodes of the Holy Spirit.

Deign, O Lord, by the grace of the Holy Spirit, to cleanse our souls of impure thoughts, to guard them intact, and to fill them with light. Thou who enlighten every man coming into this world, enlighten our hearts with the splendor of thy grace, that we might always think what is worthy of, and what is acceptable to thy majesty, and love thee sincerely. Through Christ our Lord. Amen.

To ask for purity

Sear, O Lord, our consciences and our hearts with the fire of the Holy Spirit that we might serve thee in chastity of body and please thee in purity of heart.

Break, O Lord, the chains of our sins, and that we might offer thee the sacrifice of praise in absolute freedom and purity of spirit; restore us to that state first bestowed on us, and save us by thy mercy, Thou who, by thy mercy, hast already deigned to save us by thy grace.

O Lord, our help and protection, come to our aid, and by the strength of modesty and a renewal of chastity, make our hearts and our flesh once again flourish, that through the sacrifice offered to thy mercy we might be cleansed of all temptation. Through Christ our Lord. Amen.

To ask for charity

O God, who dost turn all things to good for those who love thee, pour into our hearts the invincible affection of thy charity, that the desires aroused by thy inspiration might not be altered by any temptation.

O Lord, we beseech thee, may the grace of the Holy Spirit enlighten our hearts, and with the sweetness of perfect charity, abundantly comfort them. Through Christ our Lord. Amen.

Invocation of the Holy Spirit

O Holy Spirit, guest enduring of my soul, remain with me, and make me able to remain always with Thee.

Oblation

Eternal, Divine Spirit, I offer thee all the prayers of the Virgin Mary and of the Apostles gathered in the cenacle, and to these I unite all my prayers, beseeching thee to come as soon as possible to renew the face of the earth.

Prayer to the Holy Spirit
(of St. Catherine of Siena)

O Holy Spirit, come into my heart. – By thy power draw it to thee, true God. – Grant me charity with reverence, – guard me, O Christ, from every evil thought. Warm and inflame me with thy most sweet love, – such that every pain seems light to me. – O my Holy Father and gracious Lord, – help me now in my every need, – Christ Love! Christ Love, Love!

Invocation of the Seven Gifts of the Holy Spirit

Spirit of Wisdom, I adore thee; Oh, make me recognize the vanity of earthly things and the importance of heavenly. *Glory be*, etc.

Spirit of Understanding, I thank thee; Oh, enlighten my mind in the faith, that it might guide me in every action. *Glory be*, etc.

Spirit of Counsel, I praise thee; Oh, make me ever docile to thy holy inspirations. *Glory be*, etc.

Spirit of Fortitude, I bless thee; Oh, make me invincible in the face of temptation and to the enemies of my soul. *Glory be*, etc.

Spirit of Knowledge, I glorify thee; Oh, help my mind to study only and always for the glory of the Lord. *Glory be*, etc.

Spirit of Godliness, I pray thee the grace that my prayers be more fervent and recollected. *Glory be*, etc.

Spirit of Holy Fear, I love thee; Oh, make me always remember the presence of God to love Him above all things.

Prayer

O Holy Spirit who, on the day of Pentecost, didst with thy light enlighten and with heavenly fire didst inflame the disciples of Christ: were there ever need of that light and fire that comes forth from thee, it is surely now when the darkness of error blinds the mind, and the cold of indifference freezes the heart. We, therefore, O Eternal Love, because of our pressing need for thy help, have recourse to thy omnipotent goodness, and we implore thee to come as soon as possible to renew the face of this earth in misery.

Come, then, O Holy Spirit, and with thy divine splendors illumine the many souls blinded by the false maxims of the world. Come, and with the fire of thy love, enkindle, and with fervor, fill so many frozen souls. Come, and with the outpouring of thy sevenfold gift, sanctify the redeemed. Come, come, demolish and scatter the kingdom of Satan; bring to be a new era of faith and grace, and make the holy kingdom of God triumph across the earth. Amen.

List of Illustrations

About the Author

The author, Don Dolindo Ruotolo, Franciscan Tertiary, was born in Naples, October 6, 1882.

Ordained priest at a very early age, he lived his priesthood in an uninterrupted, intense, sacrificial testimony to God: in the Church which he loved heroically, and among souls for whom he expended the last energies of his poor health.

He wrote colossal commentaries and meditations on Sacred Scripture which have enjoyed enthusiastic praise, but also met strong criticism... But his masterpiece was an anthology of thoughts and reflections. Composed extemporaneously during contemplative moments of prayer and recollection, these analogies and reflections, like silent seeds so productive of incalculable good, have brought immense comfort to thousands and thousands of souls.

Until the very last days of a long life, he lived more than ever at the service of souls and of the world, surviving on next to nothing materially. He led a life consisting solely in a continuous and heroic sacrifice of intense pain, which up to the very end, did not prevent him from leaving his home in order to comfort the sick. A paralytic himself, and literally doubled

 over in pain, his legs were so bent and arthritic that his every step could not have been other than agony....

He died a holy death, November 19, 1970. The cause of his beatification has been opened.

A Selection of Books from the Academy of the Immaculate

A Month with Mary *Daily Meditations for a Profound Reform of the Heart in the School of Mary* by Don Dolindo Ruotolo This little book was written by a holy Italian priest Father Dolindo Ruotolo (1882-1970). Originally written as spiritual thoughts to his spiritual daughter, the work is comprised of thirty-one meditations for the month of May. The month of Mary is the month of *a profound reform of heart:* we must leave ourselves and adorn ourselves with every virtue and every spiritual good.

Jesus Our Eucharistic Love *by Fr. Stefano Manelli, FI* A treasure of Eucharistic devotional writings and examples from the saints showing their stirring Eucharistic love and devotion. A valuable aid for reading meditatively before the Blessed Sacrament.

Who is Mary? *by Fr. Gabriele M. Pellettieri, FI* This book is a concise Marian catechism presented in a question/answer format. In this little work of love and scholarship the sweet mystery of Mary is unveiled in all its beauty and simplicity. It is a very helpful resource both for those who want to know the truth about Mary and for those who want to instruct others.

Padre Pio of Pietrelcina *by Fr. Stefano Manelli, FI* This 144 page popular life of Padre Pio is packed with details about his life, spirituality, and charisms, by one who knew the Padre intimately. The author turned to Padre Pio for guidance in establishing a new Community, the Franciscans of the Immaculate.

Devotion to Our Lady *by Fr. Stefano M. Manelli, FI* This book is a must for all those who desire to know the beauty and value of Marian devotion and want to increase their fervent love towards their heavenly Mother. Since it draws abundantly from the examples and writings of the saints, it offers the devotee a very concrete and practical aid for living out a truly Marian life.

Do You Know Our Lady *by Rev. Mother Francesca Perillo, FI* This handy treatise (125 pages) covers the many rich references to Mary, as prefigured in the Old Testament women and prophecies and as found in the New Testament from the Annunciation to Pentecost. Mary's role is seen ever beside her Divine Son, and the author shows how Scripture supports Mary's role as Mediatrix of all Graces. Though scripture scholars can read it with profit, it is an easy read for everyone. Every Marian devotee should have a copy for quick reference.

Come Follow Me *by Fr. Stefano Manelli, FI* A book directed to any young person contemplating a religious vocation. Informative, with many inspiring illustrations and words from the lives and writings of the saints on the challenging vocation of total dedication in following Christ and His Immaculate Mother through the three vows of religion.

St. Maximilian Kolbe Martyr of Charity – Pneumatolgist *by Fr. Peter Damian Fehlner, FI* A scholarly study of St. Maximilian's teaching on the Holy Spirit and Our Lady; focus of contemporary criticism of the Saint and of his Marian program of life and thought, by both conservatives as well as liberals. The author, being a prominent Kolbe scholar, shows how Kolbe's perspectives are in full continuity with those of St. Francis and the great Franciscan doctors of the Church. Thoroughly documented with extensive bibliography.

Saints And Marian Shrine Series
Edited by Bro. Francis Mary, FI

Padre Pio - The Wonder Worker The latest on this popular Saint of our times including the two inspirational homilies given by Pope John Paul II during the beatification celebration in Rome. The first part of the book is a short biography. The second is on his spirituality, charisms, apostolate of the confessional, and his great works of charity.

A Handbook on Guadalupe   This well researched book on Guadalupe contains 40 topical chapters by leading experts on Guadalupe with new insights and the latest scientific findings. A number of chapters deal with Our Lady's role as the patroness of the pro-life movement. Well illustrated.

Kolbe   *Saint of the Immaculata*   Of all the books in the Marian Saints and Shrines series, this one is the most controversial and thus the most needed in order to do justice to the Saint, whom Pope John Paul II spoke of as "the Saint of our difficult century [twentieth]." Is it true, as reported in a PBS documentary, that the Saint was anti-Semitic? What is the reason behind misrepresenting this great modern day Saint? Is a famous mariologist right in accusing the Saint of being in error by holding that Mary is the Mediatrix of all Graces? The book has over 35 chapters by over ten authors, giving an in-depth view of one of the greatest Marian Saints of all times.

For a complete listing of books, tapes and CD's from the Academy of the Immaculate please refer to our catalog. Request a free catalog by email, letter, or phone via the contact information for the Academy of the Immaculate.

THE ACADEMY OF THE IMMACULATE

The Academy of the Immaculate, founded in 1992, is inspired by and based on a project of St. Maximilian Kolbe (never realized by the Saint because of his death by martyrdom at the age of 47, August 14, 1941). Among its goals the Academy seeks to promote at every level the study of the Mystery of the Immaculate Conception and the universal maternal mediation of the Virgin Mother of God, and to sponsor publication and dissemination of the fruits of this research in every way possible.

The Academy of the Immaculate is a non-profit religious-charitable organization of the Roman Catholic Church, incorporated under the laws of the Commonwealth of Massachusetts, with its central office at Our Lady's Chapel, POB 3003, New Bedford, MA 02741-3003.

AcademyoftheImmaculate.com

Special rates are available with 25% to 60% discount depending on the number of books, plus postage. For ordering books and further information on rates to book stores, schools and parishes: *Academy of the Immaculate, P.O. Box 3003, New Bedford, MA 02741,* Phone *(888)90. MARIA [888.90.62742],* E-mail *academy@marymediatrix.com.* Quotations on bulk rates by the box, shipped directly from the printery, contact: *Franciscans of the Immaculate, P.O. Box 3003, New Bedford, MA 02741, (508)996-8274,* E-mail: *fi-academy@marymediatrix.com.* Website: *www.marymediatrix.com.*